£4

Neil Gunn

HIGHLAND PACK

With drawings by
Keith Henderson

RICHARD DREW PUBLISHING
GLASGOW

First published 1939 by Faber and Faber Ltd

This edition first published 1989 by
Richard Drew Publishing Ltd
6 Clairmont Gardens, Glasgow G3 7LW
Scotland

Foreword © Dairmid Gunn 1989

The publisher acknowledges the financial
assistance of the Scottish Arts Council in the
publication of this book.

British Library Cataloguing in Publication Data

Gunn, Neil M. (Neil Miller), 1891-1973
    Highland pack,
    I. Title
    823'.912[F]

    ISBN 0-86267-264-3

Printed and bound in Great Britain

For
THE GARDENER

Acknowledgements

Acknowledgements are also made to the *Glasgow Herald* and to the *S.M.T.* (now *Scotland's*) *Magazine* for having first published one or more of these country notes and to *Chamber's Journal* for parts of the final chapters describing the trip to Bernera and the Flannan Isles.

Foreword

". . . When I was asked to consider writing a personal book on the Highlands I was oddly embarrassed for, as there is hardly a corner of that wide and varied area which does not contain for me some memorable experience, I would scarcely know where to begin, what to stress." So writes Neil Gunn, one of Scotland's most distinguished 20th century authors, in his introduction to this collection of essays. His claim of a wide knowledge of the Highlands of Scotland is easily substantiated. Nearly all of his many novels are set in the Highlands, some with clear associations with identifiable parts of this most beautiful region of Scotland. By a strange coincidence "The Shadow", the novel that preceded this book in the Scottish Collection, is set in the same blessed patch of land as the majority of these essays. The area is the hill country near the small county town of Dingwall in Ross and Cromarty. From the front of the farm house that he had rented shortly before the War Gunn could enjoy magnificent views to the South and West of glen, hill and mountains. Behind the house the land rose steeply, and grassland quickly became merged with moor and sky. An idyllic spot for a writer to spend his creative years.

It is perhaps a strange irony that the years Gunn spent near Dingwall were those of the War and the depressing period immediately after that great world conflict. For Gunn, for whom war was terrible and real, the countryside in one form or another presented the antithesis to all the horrible fare of global strife — death, destruction and displaced people. The essays produced over a period of time, and not consciously written with a collection in mind, can be read with pleasure simply as a countryman's notes, following, as such observations generally do, the pattern imposed on the land by the changing seasons. Each essay has its own interest and can stand proudly alone as one piece in a comprehensive descriptive mosaic of the Highlands. Gunn's countryman's eye seems to have missed nothing in nature's endless pageant — the sad and lingering beauty of December flowers, the breathless speed of a mountain hare, the mystery of a flight of wild geese or duck overhead, the roar of a tractor in a field or a curling stone on a frozen loch, the wonder invoked by a robin on an apple bough against the new moon or a hoodie crow on a tree over a dying lamb. It's all there and the author can rightly claim to be a packman or pedlar of fascinating and inviting wares for the reader from this "Highland Pack".

For those subjected to the tribulations of War and its aftermath the essays had a special significance. Even now, they are life enhancing and, above all, restorative. In the essay "Mountain Calendar" written at the beginning of the War he juxtaposes the fear of Armageddon that haunts many people with a charmingly prosaic description of his wife's daily round in house and garden. Against some speculative talk on the threat of dark ages and the possible formation of little isolated groups to take delight in the stars, sunlight, various arts, religious experience and the simple goodness of fellowship there is a comforting allusion to his wife, the gardener. "Meantime, the gardener reports that the green shoots of her snowdrops, crocuses, scillas and hyacinths are well above the grey frost, confident of the sun that will blow them into blossom." The enchanting background of hill and moor is a perfect foil for Gunn's imaginative musings. It is as though at times he was accompanied on his walks by such poets as Wordsworth, of whom he was a great admirer, and the Austrian Rainer Maria Rilke. In "The Gentle Rain from Heaven" there is the balance of the actual and the figurative. "I fancy I can hear the ground drinking in the rain, drinking it in with a myriad of dry upturned mouths like the mouths of lambs . . . and the rain is coming straight down, not pelting but steady and even, in a monotony that is like a consumated ecstasy", and in another plane. "And then Rilke's poetry fell like rain from heaven upon the arid place beneath . . . and down the rain falls, gently over the body and seeping deeply into the blood."

Although in this collection Gunn alludes to other writers and composers, his reflections are subtly contained in the descriptions of what he sees and hears on hill and moor and at sea. Indeed the climax to the book is a remarkable essay on ferrying sheep, land animals, across the sea to a Hebridean island, the Promised Land. The collection gives the imaginative reader much on which to ponder. In his introduction Gunn hopes that the virtue of the book will not be lost during the years when the threat of war has truly receded. He implies that in an increasingly materialistic age there has never been a greater need for the peace and contemplation that a life in the country can provide and the appreciation of the value of such a life. It is no accident that he inscribes this book to his wife, "the gardener", whose gentle companionship and quiet presence in house and garden meant so much to him. It seems appropriate, therefore, to end this short foreword with the final sentence of Voltaire's Candide, when the world-weary Candide, tired of listening to the false optimism of the ever pontificating Pangloss, says, "That's true enough, but we must go and work in the garden."

DAIRMID GUNN

Introduction

Most of these notes on country life appeared under a pseudonym in the pages of *The Scots Magazine* during the early years of the last war. The editor, Dr. J. B. Salmond, thought that something of the kind might interest his readers in those critical months when the personal life, the simple ways of living as we had known them in our part of the world, were in danger of being submerged. Their first general title, "Memories of the Month", probably describes them accurately enough, for they were essentially impressions from facts rather than objective descriptions of any kind of natural history observed by the scientific eye. Mostly they are concerned with ordinary day-to-day happenings around a farmhouse in the Highlands, though occasionally they touch on excursions to remote places, to the Hebrides, to the northern and western seas and the decks of fishing-boats. When they were being written nothing could have been further from my mind than the thought of gathering them into a book; yet when I was asked to consider writing a personal book on the Highlands I was oddly embarrassed for, as there is hardly a corner of that wide and varied area which does not contain for me some memorable experience, I would scarcely know where to begin, what to stress. Yet I should like to write such a book were it but in simple gratitude for having been born and permitted to spend nearly all my life there. Possibly at the best, then, the result for a short book could only be a matter of selection of incident or place, bits and pieces that might give an impression of a wider and richer realm. Here, perhaps, impressionism, that painter's

word, is the only word; though even it is conditioned, restricted, by the background of war.

I have a sudden remote memory of a packman arriving at a
Highland door with the great round pack on his back. Cour-
teously the woman of the house invites him in and young eyes
wait, brighter than the eyes of squirrels, while elderly talk goes
on and the black iron kettle is swung in over the peat fire. The
talk is talk of the world, of what is happening in this place or
that, of crops and fishings, marriages and births, death and the
weather, but always with a pair of keen humorous eyes lifting
from hands that pause so tantalizingly in the lengthy process of
opening the pack.

For there were no Protected Areas in the Highlands in those
days. When these notes were being written, how welcome the
old packman would have been among us — and not solely for
his news; though there again, what could even the brightest
eyes have done, with every last penny in a warm hand, without
coupons? And would the fingers of the packman have dallied
so tantalizingly with the knots, his eyes have had so cunning a
humour, if the hidden stuffs within had lost their silken sheen,
their vivid colours?

In our day we have to forage deep for what buried treasure
may have been left in the pack. The colour and expectancy have
taken refuge in the flower by the doorstep or in the ditch. The
knots are not so obviously where they were. Perhaps a still
older pack than the packman's has to be dug out of somewhere.
Tentatively we make what simple beginnings we can, and in
this matter, more properly, it may be, on things around the
doorstep than with eyes lifted in a dumb stare on the ends of
the earth.

In these pages, time drifts somewhat uncertainly, like the
weather, from wintry blossoms and spring frosts, through the
long daylight of our northern summers, to the harvesting of
the crops. Parts of the original writing had to be cut and

INTRODUCTION

trimmed, for repetition inevitably creeps in, again like the weather, over recurring months. For the rest I can but hope that whatever virtue they held for a time when personal life and its heritage were being imminently threatened may not have been lost for a time when the threat, if apparently less immediate, is hardly less profound.

NEIL GUNN

Contents

CONTENTS

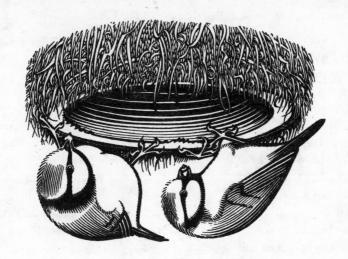

December Flowers

"Listen to this," she said, and from the correspondence page of one of the popular Sunday newspapers she read a man's boast of the number of flowers he had blooming in his Devon garden in the first week of December. "If I can't beat that," and she hurriedly left the room. Now we live in a valley in Ross-shire, and, though we are on the sunny side, still it's a long way north of Devon. Experience should have taught me, however, never to say "Nonsense" or "Impossible" when talking to a gardener. By her expression when she returned I saw at once that the Devon man must be running hard for a place. From a slip of paper she read: "Primrose, scabious, aubrietia, marigold, michaelmas daisy, roses, primula wanda, carnation, rock rose, thrift, jessamine, rock violet, montbretia, autumn gentian, pink campion, larkspur, nasturtiums, catmint, a pulchella (forget its Christian name), speedwell, pansies, hot pokers, and rose of sharon."

"I don't believe a word of it," I said, throwing caution to the winds. I paid, of course, by being led around. The list was correct, even if some of the blooms appeared to me to be such bedraggled ghosts of themselves that they were hardly worth recording. Yet the show of marigolds was really very strong, and of the others curiously enough the primroses and the campions were most profuse, those wild, delicate woodland flowers. We have had considerable experience of primroses in December. My theory at the beginning was that if you go out into the woods and take the wild ones home and plant them in sheltered, fertile ground, then you may expect them to be a little amazed and come up at the wrong time, but after a year or two they are bound to fall back into their natural rhythm. Yet I must confess that after ten years in our last house, pale, pale yellow blooms still smiled upon us in drear December, and after three winters here the campion and the primrose salute us, if not with robust vigour, at least with an engaging shyness.

It has, of course, been a remarkably open autumn. Both in the northern and western Highlands week followed week of perfect weather. It may have been that the condition of the world gave to days of stillness and colour a memorable beauty. I have one particular memory of Rogie Falls, between Contin and Garve, on an overcast day, with low clouds threatening rain. Suddenly as we came among the birches a voice cried: "Ah, there's the sun!" We got out of the car to welcome it, and it was only after I had deliberately looked up that I observed the sky had not changed. The heart-lifting effect of sunlight had come entirely from the golden glory of the birches. They glowed, and we walked like strangers in a world of light.

The same weather ripened the harvests. I have never known farmers so busy or their workers so keen. The need to get the harvest in haunted the mind. And the good weather held as if a hand were uplifted in divine pity. A second flowering came to the wild roses, and it was no uncommon sight to see pink or white blooms on a bush already red with hips. Here and there the whin is flowering still, a dozen or so yellow fragile blossoms on top. But that perhaps is a common enough occurrence, for an old lady has told us that "when the whin is out of flower, kissing will be out of fashion".

The leaves have now fallen and the deciduous trees stand revealed in naked stem and branch and twig. I know no better way of apprehending the essential nature of a tree than by seeing it in the evening with its myriad twigs etched clearly against the sky. A great elm thus seen on an upland, with the shadows gathering in the stillness of frost, can, if one looks long enough, induce a harking back into a condition of time and place that holds a faint necromantic dread—not wholly undesired.

A touch of odd feeling, too, can be got from the fallen leaves on a path overshadowed by trees, in this case not from sight but from smell. Although it emanates from decay, it is not unpleasant but faintly pungent and aromatic. Not death but change and transformation; and by way of variation, here is not its vision or its sound, but its scent.

Many hold that December is a dull, dreary month in the country. In a certain sense there is no doubt some truth in this, but actually each month has its own characteristic needs, and much is going on, from the shepherd who, with keel in his pocket, is visiting his breeding ewes, to the rabbit-trapper moving darkly from field to field. To-night as I came down the path towards the steading I heard what I thought was the drone of the inevitable bomber. I looked into the sky, but it was calm and clear, and not until I drew near did I identify the drone of the threshing-mill. Wonderfully alike in pitch, these two.

With the passing of standing corn and foliage and lush grass, many birds and animals have become familiar again. The brown hare, that seemed to have vanished altogether, starts from feet that wander to the boggy patches to flush a snipe. To the round wood, the woodcock have come back. The partridge flight between stubble and turnip field; ear and eye are startled by the whirring of a gorgeous cock pheasant unseen all summer. I knew all the partridge coveys, and now by counting can in some measure assess the full havoc wrought by the gun.

But the birds that have come back to our very window are the tits. Any hour of the short day they may be watched performing their acrobatics with faultless skill. And they really are worth watching—provided you have given them some small scope for display. Our apparatus is very simple. Beyond the gravel in front of our living-room grows a young cherry-tree on a green bank. From various points on this cherry-tree are suspended four half-coco-nuts and one small wire cage of animal fat. That is all. There is a way, of course, of suspending the apparatus if you wish the best results. Here is the simplest. Through the half-coco-nut drive a hole with a nail; thread a string through this hole from the outside and knot it on the inside (to the nail if you like), so that when the half-sphere hangs from the string its open face will be vertical. Let it hang at a distance of a foot or more from the selected branch. The wind, catching this cup, readily sends it swaying and revolving. In the same way, hang up the little wire box with the fat, the string being tied to the middle of the top or lid. Then wait for the tits.

Three kinds visit us: the great tit, the cole tit, and the blue tit (or tomtit), and they are all such flashing trapeze artists that birds like robins and chaffinches, whom one may have hitherto thought nimble enough, are revealed as hopelessly stiff and gauche, real country cousins, whose very colours are dull. Of course, it's all right at first, when the little cage is full of fat; cock robin can then stand on the lid and peck through the wire mesh as stolidly as chaffinch or sparrow or blackbird; but when the fat gets eaten down about an inch and the mesh keeps the beak from reaching it, then it is amusing to watch him fly at the cage from below and try to hover long enough to get one nibble. After two or three efforts he is reduced to a state of very manifest frustration. But the tit—from yards away *whoops!* and he has sent the box spinning and twisting, while, upside down, he pecks away with precision and gusto. But not for very long. He is full up, the rascal, and in his wanton game translates himself to the coco-nut by magic. Two or three swift taps and out shoot head and shoulders round the corner of the shell to see where everyone is, and back before you've rightly glimpsed the act.

A thought has swooped like a bird: if the war continues into a second December there may be no coco-nuts, no fat to spare. And the mind goes more still than it did before the bare elm-tree on the upland field.

Mountain Calendar

There is a knoll on the moor beyond the crofting land that we sometimes visit. It is not conspicuous in any way except for its four standing stones. Obviously it was an important spot in prehistoric days, and we never fail to be impressed by the nature and the vast extent of the view obtained from its gentle summit. For it not only takes in great mountain ranges, but overlooks the fertile valleys on their way to the sea. Chance led me on the shortest day of the year to stand amid the four stones as the sun was setting, and suddenly it came upon me how easy it would be for the simplest shepherd of prehistoric times to tell fairly accurately from the setting sun the time of the year. The sun was going down on a mountain that was higher than any to the south of it. Farther south than that summit the sun never sets. My eye could stare without much discomfort at the round molten ball with its flickering black shadow. From now onwards the sun will set farther west. The peaks that stretch in an arc through west to north-west, where the sun sets in the height of summer, could readily be used as a sort of notch-board, and certainly one not likely to be mislaid. It may be interesting to watch for the months from the standing stones.

A wise divine, whom I asked about these stones, told me that they were known to old Gaelic inhabitants as *Na Daoine Gòrach*, meaning The Foolish Men. From his smile I understood his hidden meaning, for we have occasionally discussed antiquities and place-names. The early Christians had undoubtedly an understanding of the human mind in fellowship that went very deep. Whatever the original form of worship or rite at the standing stones, the men of the new faith did not as a rule attack it with brutal intolerance in an effort at utter annihilation. Sometimes they simply put a cross on the stone, or reared a new stone in the shape of a cross. But in any case, and in the new light, these old stones were just foolish stones. Indeed they do rather look to-day like four old foolish men or bodachs. And once you have seen them like that, fellowship is not lost, it is deepened. We are one with them. What is lost is animosity.

"Ah," says the cattleman as we leaned on the gate, "how times have changed! In my young days we would be preparing for a whole week for the New Year. What fun there would be! Now no-one is preparing. It's nothing."

Some think that we are entering upon a new period of the dark ages. Once again groups may form, little isolated groups, to take delight in the stars, in sunlight, in various arts, in religious experience, in birds, in trees, in darkness, in things made by man's hand, in flowers, and above all in the simple goodness of fellowship.

Meantime the gardener reports that the green shoots of her snowdrops, crocuses, scillas, and hyacinths are well above the grey frost, confident of the sun that will blow them into blossom. And how certain it is that the sun, whom the folk of the standing stones may have worshipped, will not betray their confidence.

The Frightened Worm

Going up the field from the back of the house I met one of the ploughmen who assured me that the soil was frozen solid for over a foot down. In the shadows the old grass was noisy to the feet and even in the sun bright crystals could be shed in a shower: a lovely invigorating morning, windless and still, as if the long spell of frost had forgotten how to end. Lest we should ever grow tired of talking of the weather, nature has provided us with three main brands: fine weather, stormy weather, and broken weather; and now and then each has an innings which gathers about it a fatal air as though the gods had got into a trance and could no longer move or even wink an eyelid. It is the kind of mood which sometimes affects the Highlander himself, coming from he hardly knows where and staying with him beyond reason. The ploughman's voice was quiet and resigned, for work was already behind.

At the top of the field there is a grassy bank, on top of the bank a wire fence, and beyond the fence stretched the next field still unmarked by the plough. I sit down on the bank to enjoy the sun, for the slope faces south and the sun is well above the opposing ridge of the glen.

Whatever mindlessness I had fallen into, I am presently startled, and experience, quite literally, a clutch of fear. It was as

24

if a hand had knocked twice on an other-world or underworld door; yet it wasn't a knock so much as a hard swift scrape of nails, something more peremptory than a knock and more ominous. In a couple of moments I am looking over at the shallow ravine made by a small burn; old trees grow along it and doubtless the cause of the mysterious sounds would be found there. I remain absolutely still, and now slightly ashamed of the fear, of having, as it were, been caught off guard. But I am wary and await the emergence of beady eyes and a stealthy body with complete control. The tension in the frosted air is the tension of an invisible eardrum listening beyond silence; the morning is peaceful, the sun in its heaven. But when the sounds are repeated, I leap to my feet as if I had been bitten by a snake and find myself actually dusting the seat of my trousers in an effort to dust the bite off while my eyes stare at the spot on which I had been resting. For it was from that spot that the peremptory summons had come, from underneath the spot, from beneath the frozen ground.

I realize, of course, that I have been a victim of the old serpent fear, but that does not help at the moment, for the harsh scraping sounds had been real enough. Of that there could be no doubt. As I can think of no possible cause, I watch and listen.

The red tip comes up out of the frozen earth like the shoot of a frenzied plant; it grows, it reaches out and over, it sways; it comes pouring out and after four inches it is still coming. If the frost has narrowed the hole, the worm has thinned itself accordingly, but now it is all out and travelling fast, plainly mad with fear. As a boy I have often hunted worms for a Highland burn in spate, but never have I seen a worm move as this worm moves. Then I see that its body is actually in a cold froth of fear. Glistening rings of real froth are left behind on the stiff grass blades. At the foot of the bank there is a sheer drop of nine or ten inches. Its head comes over this miniature precipice, reaches out, reaches for a wild new hold on space, but cannot find it, yet cannot stop; it pours itself out into space until what is left of its body on earth can no longer keep hold and the full five inches of worm fall over the precipice.

But in no time the folds have disentangled themselves and the worm is off. I follow it until at last it crawls into the head of a tuft of grass that has been shorn close and there it tries to bury itself among the tough shoots. But even these seem frozen stiff and I can still see its red body resting beneath the oozing froth that glistens in the sunlight.

During the latter part of the worm's journey, my mind had conjured up its own picture of what had happened in that dark underground world. Many times I have had to hunt a mole that has been poking up bulbs in the rockery and, not content with such idle sport, has set its rash of hills upon the lawn. Extraordinary, in such circumstances, the sense of frustration and anger which this remarkable creature can arouse in even the most kind-hearted of gardeners. However, on this frosty morning it seemed as though I suddenly knew what the worm experienced when it heard or felt the mole coming, when the tremor reached it from these pink forefeet that like two shovels put the earth off a pink snout as a boat puts the green sea. The moment's paralysing fear, the race in the dark underworld, the frozen earth above, then an old passageway still open, the thrust up, the squeezing past the iron-bound corners, up and still up, until —the nail-armoured shovels resound in defeat against the frozen crust. . . .

I had somehow never thought of anything like that happening to worms in their country; and on that sunlit sparkling morning, when the drone of an enemy bomber could have been heard miles away, it seemed so remarkable that the memory of it remained with me.

I cannot help adding, on re-reading the casual reference to "the old serpent fear", that some days afterwards I was hunting out forgotten papers from a cupboard in the hope (it never quite dies) of finding what I was looking for. Actually I came on the manuscript of what in those youthful days I would have called a poem. It was entitled "The Serpent", but though I hunt my mind now for a particular serpent I cannot recall it; yet what does astonish me is the number of serpents, adders, which do come to memory, vivid with attendant circumstance, right from those of early boyhood to the one, over two feet long, which the gamekeeper killed when we were fishing a salmon beat on the Conon last July. But perhaps I am a little astonished too at the way youth had of turning from the vivid primitive fears in order to be "poetic" about them:

> Outpouring from an earth
> Close-bound by antique roots
> Of blackened heather runts
> Whose high green shoots
> Lifting frail buds of birth
> Shiver
> As your cold coils meet
> Their anguished feet.

> Outpouring from my mind
> Dark-bound by primal fears
> Your arrowy diamond head
> In glittering spell uprears
> Uprears
>   and sways
>   and dips
> Feeling among the flowers
> Whole shivering hours.

It is at least satisfactory to note that when the serpent was behaving in this way, the heather runts would in fact have been lifting frail buds of birth.

The Weasel

Moments of astonishment can haunt one corner of a field like a covey of partridges. Here are two which occurred within a few yards of that spot where I watched the flight of the terrified worm. The first has to do with a weasel, the second with a wild duck.

The keeper had been up towards the moor and through the whin scrub after rabbits. Returning in the dusk with a bagful, he sat down by the elms to have a rest and a smoke. Perhaps only those who have carried, say, five or six white hares for a mile or two after a combined shoot can realize how a bag of game bites into the shoulder. (I wonder how many have let a hare go by rather than add to the strangling burden?) Anyway, the keeper so enjoyed his pipe, sitting there in the deepening twilight, that he decided he might prolong his rest and lighten his burden by gutting the rabbits on the spot. In addition to the rabbits he had shot one weasel and was taking it home in the bag for the vermin "larder". So presently he got up, undid his swollen bag, and, turning it upside down, emptied its contents at his feet. The dead rabbits flocked and slumped, but the weasel—the weasel had a different motion altogether, it came up through the rabbits, it went over them, it reached the earth and now, before the keeper's eyes, was moving away. His gun was beside him; he could have picked the gun up and shot the weasel for it went quite a distance before it found cover, but he could not move. "I stood like a fool," he said; "I couldn't move." From the sound of his voice you knew that this was one of the most astonishing things that had ever happened to him. He had shot the weasel "stone dead". "Extraordinary, wasn't it?" Anyone listening to the keeper always smiles, as though down among the dark fibres of being the tenacity of life in a weasel is secretively and somewhat comfortingly understood.

The Wild Duck

Wild duck feed at night. They come in from the firth in the deep gloaming, flighting towards the stubble fields. They generally follow the same course, and if there is water about—say, the water in a burn—a sportsman can take his stance at a particular spot with confidence. For many, this flighting of wild duck and wild geese in the twilight of night and of morning provides the supreme sport. No outing on "the twelfth", no salmon pool, no deer stalk even, can offer anything comparable. But here we are dealing with the imponderables of loneliness in the grey light by a northern firth when influences, deeper than the daylight knows of, isolate a man, cut him off from all gregarious living, and let him see that this individual body, such as it strangely is, squatting in cold and what would normally be high discomfort behind a bush or a bank, with eyes on a grey sky, is the only thing he can be half sure of and more than half uncertain. And if that sounds like dubious arithmetic, put it down to the totality of mystery which is always greater than the sum of its solid parts. For in that isolation there is yet a communion with elementals which no school book has so far recorded nor political ideology taken into account. But as no man can be "told" about it, let us go back to the wild duck.

Just through the fence and beyond the bank where the worm raced for its red life, there were, last year, a dozen stacks of barley. The wild duck had searched them out and the shepherd in his round had become aware of the fact. So one evening he sat in wait. He shot three mallard and a duck and then, after waiting "for about another quarter of an hour", decided that the flight was over, for it does not last very long. Having picked up his four birds by the legs, he went walking along by the fence towards the gate. A moon had come up and in the dim light his keen eyes could see quite a distance. When he came to the gate he dropped the ducks and broke his gun in order to take the cartridges out. He had the cartridges in his hand when he heard a scuffle at his feet. This startled him, and then he saw that one of the ducks was moving, it was on its feet; its wings flapped, it had taken off; it was flying away down the field below him. Long after it had melted into the night he was still standing quite still with the cartridges in his hand.

I have heard him tell the story more than once.

Sometimes it sounds as though in such a moment of surprise a new and astonishing aspect of life is revealed, a new dimension even, something beyond the actual happening itself, so that one never quite ceases to marvel at it.

The Wild Goose

Having mentioned wild geese, I am tempted to record an unusual happening which has stuck in my own mind. Recently the gardener had to pay a visit to a croft house up on the edge of the moor and I went with her. Where there is a crofting area the moors and the mountains are usually not far away; usually also there is a lot of light about and singing larks; and space itself, of which there is more than the eye can readily encompass, is yet as it were parcelled out into smallness and intimacy. The cow is nearly human and the hens lay when they feel like it, which is not often. The dog comes barking and wagging his tail equally furiously; and out of sheer jealousy the dog on the next croft barks back. The child stares. The cat pays no attention. And the cock struts and *kok-koks* with the fine high-stepping action of outraged dignity.

Now the croft wife and my own can talk for a very long time. Like sportsmen, they have their own way of covering a lot of ground. If I truthfully add that the small croft garden is about the neatest and most colourful I have seen, I may not be saying much to those who have so often looked in vain for any kind of croft garden, but by that very token, in this particular case, I may be saying enough. Anyway, I know I have ample time to wander around and see what the year is busy about in the way of wild life. It is rather like turning the page of a book for what is happening next and now, and there is always the lucky chance of a vivid illustration—a lark's nest, a hare in its form, the rabbit you can put a hand on if you know how to circle its tuft of grass—with which to interrupt the gardener's news; though interrupt her it always does, for many people with excellent eyes find great difficulty in seeing the hare. (When she does see it, she always hauls me away in silence and with speed.)

On this occasion I was estimating the effectiveness of a rabbit-trapper's work, trying to read from the signs not only the man's knowledge but the kind of hands he had, when I heard a gun go off—then a second shot—both barrels—away along the crest of the moor towards wild swampy ground which in the wet season achieves a couple of respectable lochans. Then I saw the wild geese, about a dozen of them.

They were coming towards me—and passed almost over-head, making for the firth, a haunt of greylags. I suspected poachers (as it turned out, I was right) and wondered if they had got any. The birds above had fallen into an arrow forma-tion, even if it tended to waver a trifle—and no wonder. I was watching them very carefully for any sign of a hit but could detect none. The distance a wounded bird will fly is often very remarkable. They were now well away towards the firth and going strong, when one of them spoke.

Let me say that up in this crofting world sounds carry an

incredible distance on a still day, even farther than they carry over sea-water in the quiet of the night, as if the gentle slope of the ground were a vast sounding-board. (So it seems, anyhow, when half a mile away I can hear feminine farewells at a croft door.) I mention this because the voice of the goose was not loud; it was quiet but anxious. It was the anxiety in the voice that held me. I have heard flying geese talking among themselves too often in too many places, in daylight and moonlight, not to know the general tone of their discourse. Sometimes that anxious note will creep in when the whole gaggle grows uncertain in its flight, as though some lusty young fellow were disputing the old man's sense of direction among the hills. At such a moment, the formation will break and swirl as if these sure creatures of the wild were no more than a mass of plantation rooks. Not that the old man pays much attention: he steers a point or two north and heads on for he knows the way, and the last you see of them they are tailing in behind him on either side. Now though the many voices during the mix-up may sound anxious, they are also disputatious, if not indeed querulous.

But this voice was not uplifted, it was quiet. In such a voice a young man might say to his fellows: "I'm done, boys; I can't go any farther."

At once the others answered. For it was clearly and entirely the wrong place to give in. They yattered to him and their voices were strangely liquid and sweet and urgent.

I waited with a feeling of absolute suspense. The conversation continued for a few moments, then one of the geese left the formation. I saw him dropping away, then turning into the wind as he came down to land in a wide, slow, beautiful curve. As he passed from view, his flight was still so sure that he might himself have been a leader who had unexpectedly come upon some paradisal loch or firth.

But the others did not follow. They continued straight on

34

their way without the slightest suggestion of hesitation or devi-
ation. Indeed their long necks seemed outthrust more ardently
than ever. But their voices lifted a little, and though I have
always been a trifle uncomfortable over the attribution of
human feelings to bird or beast, it struck me in that moment
with a clear conviction of certainty that they were crying their
hail and farewell.

When the gardener appeared I told her what had happened
and we set off down the slopes, through hedge and fence and
watercourse, to find the greylag. It is only at such a time that
you realize how intricately broken-up may be a hillside which
from a distance looks smooth enough. The gardener was beginning to have vague doubts, and I was wondering myself if the
bird had waddled into some cover, when I saw at the upper
edge of a small field what looked like any other grey stone. But
there was a whiteness of one part that no weathered stone has on
our hillside.

The goose was quite dead and, judging from how it lay, I
knew that it had fallen the last few yards like a stone. There
were three drops of blood on the white and the body was warm.

It weighed just on seven and a half pounds. Subsequent ex-
amination showed that at least two pellets of shot had pene-
trated through the very deep flesh of the breast right to the bone.

It must have flown nearly a mile before that conversation
took place which has remained so clearly in my mind.

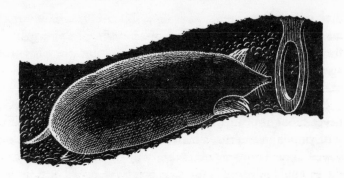

The Mole-catcher

The mole must have got into the news, for when I went across one of the low fields the other evening to where the mole-catcher was busy setting his traps he asked me if I had listened in to a broadcast by an English mole-catcher last night. I hadn't, and he proceeded to tell me that the Englishman had said that once out of forty traps he had taken forty moles. "I have never done anything like that," he admitted. "My best is fourteen out of fifteen traps." I remembered some of the lush lands in the southern counties of England and suggested that a lot must depend on the number of moles about. A mort of moles finding plenty of food would become fat and unsuspecting, and accordingly forty out of forty might be less of a feat in the south than fourteen out of fifteen in the north where the mole from necessity might be a warier animal. He spat on the small ball of earth in his left palm and then kneaded it with his right thumb.

"There may be something in that," he allowed, as his eyes lifted and looked away. His eyes were an impersonal greeny-grey, like glass or shallow sea-water. His face was lean and his hair neither fair nor dark, but somewhere in between, as the dusk comes between day and night. The kneading of his spittle into the earth had held my eye, and I was vaguely haunted by the notion of a remote creative act, as if in some far primordial age this had happened before, but when or where I could not exactly remember.

Presently, as we went on talking, I thought of moles as I had never thought of them before. We stood not far from a ditch with running water and a thick low-set thorn hedge. There they stayed in the hard weather, but now, with the frost gone from the ground and spring's stir of generation and awakening life, they adventured out into the field. I could see their paths coming from the hedge, all along the earth like swollen veins. A curiously secretive underground life, this of theirs—underground, yet, as it were, not dark, for in the countryman's proverb "a mole wants no lanthorn".

"Yes," said the mole-catcher, "I think the barrel trap is the best." All the time he explained its workings I was wondering what the earth in his palm was for. The trap is like a tiny barrel, with two grooves inside, one near each end where in a real barrel the head would be slotted. But into each groove now he introduces a noose of strong twine and fixes it in position with the kneaded clay, smoothing it all round with the ball of his thumb until noose and groove disappear. From the centre of the barrel protruded internally a tiny peg of wood. Knock out the lightly held peg, and the nooses leap from the clay by the swift action of an external spring.

In the chill of the evening his face looked cold, as though a drop of water might form any moment at his nose. Easy thought about life and death held no relation to his purpose. His intelligence was calmly remote from it, inevitably distant, and his actions had a craftsman's deliberation.

Had I not been struck by the kneading of spittle and clay I should not have had any special thoughts myself, for if the mole-catcher's job is necessary at any time, to-day it is very important—for us. These swollen veins that were the moles' tracks would spread over all the field in intricate formation like the veins in a human body, and the scores of molehills would multiply into an immense rash of countless warts, until the fructifying and growth on which our lives depend would be imperilled to the point of disaster.

"See that field up there," said the mole-catcher, pointing to a twenty-five-acre field on a slope. "The year before last I took one hundred and fifty moles off it."

I nodded, for I had seen the moles impaled in long lines on the wire fencing. "How," I asked him, as his impersonal eye slowly went over the ground about our feet, "do you find your spot for setting the trap?"

"Always look out for a new run," he answered, "because that's where she is working. See this one—it ends there. I'll set the trap here."

Round his left knee he had tied a piece of rubber tubing from a motor-car tyre, and now getting down on his knee he very neatly, with his mole-spade, cut out a section of earth the size of the barrel trap, and exposed the run.

"Always make sure," he said to me, "that your trap is deep enough," as he pounded the bottom of the run with the reverse end of his spade. "Once," he continued, "I was bedding the trap when I saw her working at the end of the run—as it might be over there. She heard me hitting the earth and came back, and, before my eyes, went clean under the trap and away. It was a lesson to me."

His fingers felt each end of the exposed run to make sure the passage was clear. All his motions were slow and deliberate and precise. There was no air about him of trusting to luck or chance. To say that this intelligence which the mole was up against was cool and ruthless would be to colour it emotionally. This intelligence did not sport with moles as the old Greek gods sported with men, or, for that matter, as many think God sports with men to this day. He was not a jealous mole-catcher, this man.

When he had bedded the trap to his satisfaction he lifted some of the dislodged earth and rolled it into a rounded lump in his palms. Long bony fingers placed the lump lightly over one end of the trap. They had a delicate touch. When at last the trap was hidden without being choked, the fingers spread a final loose covering of soil against the light. Then he switched his bag round and from it drew an arrow with a white cotton rag tied to the unpointed end. Into the earth he stuck this arrow upright.

"Yes," he answered, "it is to mark the trap. You might think it would be easy to find your trap on level ground like this, but it is often not easy. Once some sheep got in and rubbed themselves against my flags and knocked them down, and it took me a long time to find all my traps, a long time."

"I thought you would see the wire of the spring above the ground fairly easily?"

"You don't. Look back."

I looked back, and here and there saw the little white flags, but could not pick up the grey wire against the old grass.

In the gathering dusk the ground, when thus looked at closely, was suddenly like the relief map of a continent. It was not a flat, dull, uninteresting corner of a field, as any casual eye like my own might hitherto have thought. A continent reduced to this scale would be no more uneven. Myriad lines of communication, tunnelling, mountains, great valleys . . .

"Do you see that big molehill over there?" He pointed to a mountain of a molehill, a veritable fortress and citadel among molehills.

"Yes," I said.

"Well, do you see where it is placed?"

"How do you mean?"

"Look at the lie of the ground. You can see it is placed on the highest spot."

My eye was not so keen as his, but when I bent down I saw that in truth here was a city set on a hill.

He nodded at my questioning surprise, and a gleam came into his eye, faint but clear. "Oh, they know what they're doing. They know all right. They put it up there so that the flood water won't reach them." There was something impersonal even in his speech. No trace of dialect thickened his meaning. Here was the voice that within a generation had turned from its rich native Gaelic into school-book English. Only the rhythm remained, quietly fluent as the land. The gleam in the eye was a tribute to the mole's wisdom. It passed like a momentary reflection of light.

I saw now the earth below the surface, from the cities of birth on the hills to the hollows where the choking water might entrap and drown. Was water the eternal enemy?

"No, water is the one thing they must have. You'll always find their runs making for water, and water indeed when a burn rises will sometimes come down their runs and do harm to the land."

When, in the darkening, I left him and from the thorn hedge turned round to have a last look he was moving over the earth with bent head. The short-sighted moles in their underground world had never seen that figure. And it seemed unlikely that even a Lewis Carroll among their philosophers could come within glimmering range of the dispassionate, but not blind, intelligence which presently paused, got down on one knee, and, taking some earth on a palm, kneaded it with spittle.

The Roaring Game

Not for many years has the small loch been frozen so deeply or for so long as it has this February. Odd afternoons were smuggled from business to "draw the bottle" or "crack an egg" with round heavy lumps of polished grey or black granite in the "roaring game" of curling. "Can you see that?" shouts the skip to the member of his team about to play the next shot. "No." "Ah well, just try and draw. That's our own and if you promote it a foot you'll do no harm. . . . Ay, take him with you! *Take him with you!* . . . Brooms up! Gr-r-reat shot!" It's a pleasant moment in an anxious match when the skip's broom salutes one's prowess.

Afterwards in the convivial inn parlour, with hot water in the jug ("Hot, not warm," said the ancient skip to the young lassie) Hitler is directly accused of having bust what would have been a certain and great bonspiel at Carsebreck. An international bonspiel to settle all our troubles (says the skip, for it's a good dram) and, faith, we would crack eggs and fill a few pot-lids to some purpose! "The same again, and see that it's *hot* this time."

The skip grows warm with reminiscence. In the old days it wasn't a case of snatching a couple of hours with a feeling of guilt. He shook his head. From morning till night the roaring game went on, with that glorious interval for hot stew, real stew, in the middle of it. Business was left to look after itself.

The gamekeeper forsook his game, the shopkeeper his shop, the farmer his farm, ay, and the very sheriff his court, so that Justice herself had to wait until this more serious communal matter had first been dealt with.

"Sweep him up!" shouted old Jock the poacher to the sheriff, and the sheriff swept for dear life. "You for a player!" roared the town clerk to the provost, who had just laid the perfect guard, and the provost looked modest as he turned for his next stone. What a tame little affair, pursued the skip, had been our last autumn "annual meeting"! Compared with what he could remember! . . . It was enough to make one wonder, right enough, what the world was coming to. It did, honestly. For he could remember five skips closeted in this very sanctum "like the Cabinet itself", for hours, choosing their teams, while outside, crowding the bar and everywhere else, men waited anxiously on their decisions. Sometimes and in devious fashion drams would find their way to the inner sanctum from those who were, as one might say, a little over-anxious; not of course that anything in the way of influencing decisions was intended. No, no, far from it! But you know how, in the press of great decisions, a good man's name may be clean forgotten. Ay, ay! It was something to be chosen a member of a rink in those days. . . .

But such as we are to-day, we did contrive a few friendly matches with neighbouring teams during this remarkable spell of ice. And I think, perhaps, I caught at least one glimpse of the ancient spirit. The loch we visited was in a pine wood and the sunlight streamed across the tree-tops from a pale blue sky, moderating the frosty air to a degree that remained invigorating yet mild.

"Man," said Uilleam to me, "it's not that I want us to beat them—but they're that keen. They must win at all costs. They're like that. They always have been here. They can't help it."

"You think I should button my jacket?"

"To the very last button," said Uilleam.

During a recent game, some specially good shots were played after an air-raid warning had sounded, and as I cast my eye around I knew that some veteran brooms would have sloped quite smartly had the need arisen.

Later, as I walked home from the bus-stop through the frost haze, with a red horizon portending a continuation of the hard weather, there was little doing in the countryside. Here a farm hand was forking turnips out of a field-pit into his cart, and there some sheep were grouping together on a strip of turnip ground that had been fenced off for their use. It was a very quiet world, and the thin covering of snow caught and reflected the fading light in a spectral beauty. Trees and bushes were dark and motionless.

Two blackbirds began scolding in some undergrowth and I know of no sounds more characteristic of a late winter afternoon in the country. I seem to have heard these sounds at such moments all through my life, and for some mysterious reason there is youth in them and vigour and promise, and they always raise a friendly smile. One seems to know why they are scolding without quite knowing it, as if the whole performance were an earnest yet wanton excess, not far removed from certain moods which have a wanton way of assailing ourselves. A sheep coughed, with a regular old man's cough, a hoast, chesty and pretty rheumy, poor fellow. His face looked very grey—though for that matter all the sheep-faces looked grey, ghost-grey. But two or three of them, pressing up against a low hedge, suddenly began to box playfully and make little leaps. They had youth on their side, however, and their elders were clearly not impressed. And then from down by the edge of the turnip field, there all at once came a handful of clear singing bird-notes, as if a few thrushes or larks were laughing together. I have rarely heard anything so unexpected, so spontaneous, so happy. It was a singing from the ground, not from trees or the air. I listened for some time but did not hear it repeated, and it was almost as though a trick had been played on me. But I knew I had got an insight into the bird-mind and found it, in a certain respect, not so vastly different from the mind of a boy I had known long ago. As I pursued my way happily tired along the hard-rutted cart road, a new sound, like the drone of an aeroplane, came down through the frosted evening. I remembered the "warning". I looked at the vacant sky. But once more it was the blessed drone of the threshing-mill.

February and the Birds

There is one annual event that never seems to stale with the years: the hearing of the first full bird's song. I don't mean the lively chattering of sparrows or yattering of starlings, heartening as these may be on a mild damp day with blinks of a living sun and promise of more to come, but the first individual song that heralds the turn of the year and has in it not a little of incantation. For it sings of spring to come, yet the memory of past springs are gathered into it. Now may be understood the meaning of Wordsworth's line: "That there hath passed away a glory from the earth"; because suddenly the glory is singing here and now to the mortal ear.

A memorable experience of this kind occurred many years ago in a wooded lane that bordered a nursery garden in the town of Inverness. It was the second day of January and the bare branches of great beeches were dark against the dawn in the sky; a soft mild morning in which one could imagine worms coming up to see what the iron frost had done to the earth. On a topmost twig, the thrush sang full-throated, its notes ringing out, clear and vibrant, over the awakening world. It was so unexpected on only the second day of the new year, and so triumphant, that the dullest mind would have been held spellbound, not merely by the rush of notes but by the unnameable promise that quivered at their core, quivered and travelled far over trees and blue smoke.

This year we had a mild few days at the end of the first week of January, and, going up the wooded path towards the moor, I was greeted for the first time by a wren's song—not quite with the full force and precision, the ringing *ran-dan-dan*, that will develop presently—but still the true song.

Round as a brown puff ball and with tidy tail cocked up, he is an engaging fellow; and friendly just now, accompanying one up the bank often for quite a distance. He runs round the tree trunks and out and in roots and grass exactly like a mouse. Once or twice we have tried to follow where he disappears to see if we could find him, but without success. One day he entered a hole in the snow against the grassy side of a bare ditch and, knowing that at least he could not come out without our seeing him, we followed up the hole under the foot of snow until we had the feeling he was probably a hundred yards away enjoying the gentle game of fooling us.

I have rarely observed so many chaffinches about, and a short time ago, coming down through the turnip field after the sun had set, I happened upon hundreds of them, twittering sweetly as with short flights they kept in front of me. I stopped and observed them fluttering about and clinging to the slender green stalks and tiny pods of the charlock. Examining the pods, I found them stripped open and cleaned of their seeds. An outside pod the bird would weigh down on to the snow and there deal with it. A roll in the field set them and the charlock against the light in the western sky.

FEBRUARY AND THE BIRDS

During that soft spell in early January, the gardener was enchanted by a visit to her lawn of two pied wagtails and what she thought were two yellow wagtails at the same time. It is, I know, not always easy at a little distance to distinguish the yellow wagtail from the grey, particularly in winter-time, as the under parts of both birds are a bright yellow. Indeed I have seen the grey wagtail, in certain fluttering movements, look more yellow than the yellow wagtail. But faced by the authorities who state that the yellow wagtail visits us exclusively in the summer, the gardener suggested that odd specimens of this graceful and beautiful bird may have acquired in our land the Highland endowment of "second sight" and so been able to foresee the unusually severe weather conditions which did in fact visit the Continent this winter!

Now in February we have a note from a correspondent in Eigg of the Inner Hebrides (which has many fascinating stories of "second sight") saying that two yellow wagtails are wintering in that delectable isle.

The first grey wagtail I ever saw was hovering (presumably amid a dance of flies) in a shaft of sunlight. I have never forgotten the perfection, in movement and colour, of that moment and still think the grey wagtail our most elegant bird.

I have read somewhere that the popular name Washerwoman (in France, *Lavandière*) belongs to the whole wagtail family from the resemblance in sound between the beating of linen on a river's edge and the beating of the tail of the bird as it trips across the floating leaves of the water lily.

And here is a conundrum from that same correspondent in Eigg: "Can you tell me which kind of bird flying overhead at night would make a noise rather like women's voices talking loudly but with a sweetness in the sound? I was lying awake and heard the voices coming out of the distance slowly and passing quickly over the house and away without much crescendo. They must have been high, I think."

Eigg came to my mind in quite another connection, too, when that short mild spell passed and the frost dug its grey nails into the ground. We had some three inches of snow at the most, and its small fine crystals made a sound underfoot very similar in kind to that which greets the feet on the Singing Sands of Eigg.

On the uplands here the snow drifted into curves of a singular purity and fascination. On an afternoon of no visible sun I found it impossible at a few yards to tell where the suave summit of a curve stopped and the infinitely faint shadow began. Line and shadow ran into each other in a glimmering light that was easy to look at and yet evaded the eyes as movement in water does. More than once in traditional Gaelic story (that of Deirdre, for example) I have come upon the similitude of blood on snow for the beauty not always of the woman. Some juniper bushes in the centre of a wood looked all bewitched, the heavy undisturbed snow curling on outer branches into fantastic tongues. Walt Disney would have delighted in them. All the trees had their own character, waiting in such an extraordinary stillness that you involuntarily listened also.

I was glad to find, too, that the trapper has not killed all the rabbits, nor the collie dog the hares, and even the two wild duck after a long absence were back in the pool in the wood. From the tracks in the snow one could tell not only the hare's speed but his dietetic intention. It was the quiet lope of an easy mind. There was a woodcock nearer the house than I've ever seen one, and the snipe had come to the running burn.

I thought of the snow in our cities, "a moment white" then churned to slush; or in foreign cities where I've seen it months old and looking like debris from a plague. Though for that matter snow does not wear well anywhere near human habitation. Perhaps it is too white, too virginal, too pure, to hold its rapture long. But it has its day or two, and particularly in the mind of the young. I can remember a small boy getting out of a warm bed and going to a window, while it was yet hardly daylight, and seeing his hope of a white world fulfilled. The thrill—and promise—of that moment!

The snow is a memory already, for on February the 8th the sun came out on as lovely and bright a morning as we'll have this spring. The gardener was appalled at the colour of the window panes. Snowdrops of three different kinds all in bloom and growing. And the aconites, which she had lost, suddenly discovered in golden petal and green frill. Ice-blackened myosotis leaves can cover anything.

Pink fingers of peony and pink fists of rhubarb opening out into tender pink hands; and here the thrusting tulip, too. But ah, everywhere, in twos and threes, in round groups, in long lines, are the spears of spring itself, stiff, at attention, but hearing afar off the blowing of their golden trumpets.

"The Innocent Brightness of a New-born Day is Lovely Yet"

I would have had to be told that the above quotation is from Wordsworth's "Intimations of Immortality", so long ago it is since I have read that remarkable poem. (Indeed, I must confess that I haven't opened Wordsworth for more years than I can remember.) I came back to it by a prompting that lies too deep for explanation, following an experience which I cannot hope to make reasonable, much less clear or vivid. Last month the earth was storm-swept, snow and thaw and frost, biting gales from north and east, and sleety penetrating sou'westers. There were occasional bright days, but under them the earth lay dead, waiting for more calamities to follow, in a human world over-laid with calamity and foreboding.

And then on a day towards the end of February, as I was coming down the farm lane, with a thorn hedge on one side and the stream that runs into the mill dam on the other, I ob-served that the green heads of the butter-burs were everywhere, on the bank, in between the bared roots of gnarled trees that overhang the water, bursting balls of a vivid freshness, bringing mortal feet and eyes to a standstill in surprise and astonishment. Something had been happening. The earth was not dead.

Small birds were in the thorn hedge, weaving from branch to branch, restless living shuttles, shedding their own quick sounds on the air. And then I found that the air itself was mild. I looked up through it at the sky. I don't remember whether the sky was clear or particularly blue, for what I saw somehow was the light in the air itself. The air was charged with this light, and the light came from the air and lay soft as thistledown on the fields. The fields were aware of it, but, as it were, gave no sign, holding to this demeanour secretively, with the solemn unwinking gaiety which Nature knows how to assume.

Well, it raised a smile, and the heart turned over like the enchanted sleeper who hears the fabled horn, and hope perhaps pushed up a green star, and it was pleasant; there was this positiveness of re-birth in an earth grown too weary of destruction and death, and that at least was something.

But that didn't end the matter. I was conscious of this light going with me down the lane, though, after all, that was natural enough, for it was everywhere. But I came to the front of the house, and the snowdrops were there, in apparently vastly greater numbers than last year. And the gravel was dry. The front door stood open. And then the curious thing happened. As I entered at the sitting-room door, I had to obey an impulse not to close it. I experienced the curious feeling that to close it would be to shut out what had been accompanying or following me. There was no suggestion of an individual presence, no classic Primavera or personification of Spring about to walk in on visible or invisible feet. Something much older, old as the rocks, old as light itself, without conscious form in my mind, just out there.

As I write this, I have a picture of a body in its lounge chair at that odd moment. Though here again I am not precise, for all

I see are the legs with the feet bent in towards the chair, in slumped stillness—quite divorced from their owner now, and belonging to that curious appointment.

This was the experience, then, that subsequently made me hunt up Wordsworth's poem.

The poem broke on me in daylight; and if passages were familiar from encountered quotation, they were no more familiar than earth and rock and spring flowers in "the innocent brightness of a new-born day". And I knew then, whether, as individuals, we are moved or not moved, in whole or in part, by the poem, that it holds a spirit as eternal as the light that came down the lane and hesitated at the front door.

Snowdrops and aconites and snow, accident and illness. Such has been the environment to our toil and national preoccupations for some time past. We were on a visit to hospital when she said to me: "What about bringing him some flowers?" This was a happy thought, for he had once expressed a theory about flowers in a man's sick-room (and he had been through the 1914 war as a youth and badly wounded). "They bring you books," he had said, "and fruit and soda siphons and all that, but the one thing folk never think of bringing to a man is flowers."

Now he is not particularly keen on flowers normally, little more so I should say than the average healthy man, but I fancied I began to see his point when I thought about it. A hospital is a place of corridors and straight lines and cleanliness and angles and regulations and fixed times. The nurses smile firmly and plot the course of events on a chart. The surgeon and the house surgeon with the sister and the nurse bear down in an upright attitude upon a body that feels like a rudderless boat, half-stove in and floating precariously. It is pushed along to an X-ray room or an operating theatre. The sprung planking is examined. Things are done to it when the mind has been blacked-out. And the eyes open to the same old lines and angles and try to read what may be hidden behind the outward assurance of the medical face.

At the best of times it is a long, wearisome business. The mind is apt to become obsessed with its own troubles. What else is there to think about or look at? It is at this moment, we were told, that the sight of flowers does a fellow good. They belong to that other world of bright sunny growing things. Capital folk, the doctors and the nurses; a marvellous institution, a hospital; but if only one could slip away to where the wind is cool on the face and the flowers growing!

We saw a few red carnations in a slender vase in a florist's window. The very thing! Colour and radiance. "I'll take those. How much, please?"

"Fourteen shillings."

Fourteen shillings! It was amusing to see the look of utter consternation on the feminine countenance.

I suppose it is hard for a gardener who studies ways and means with twopenny packets and sixpenny roots, whose passion is flower-growing, who gives away slips and cuttings and bunches, suddenly to have to face so fabulous a situation.

A few days later our snowdrops were called in to redress the balance, and right delicately they did it, for they had not been forced and spoke the true tongue of the season and told of passing snows and the certainty of summer.

But snowdrops are not enough, and I sincerely hope there will be no vague mutterings about any revolutionary need for glass or heat. However, I don't think there will, because of the strong bias to meet the season face to face, in the open air, fingers in the unprotected earth.

I observe stirrings already. There are movements in the air, for this is the first day of March and the sun has been shining, though the wind is still cold and the hills white. There has

apparently been some difficulty about getting a new pair of
trousers of the right kind. In one pair that came by post she
nearly expired laughing because she couldn't bend. It was necessary to remind her that there was a war on and things had to be
rationed. She sent them back, however.

Meanwhile I have been posted a catalogue. It is entitled
"The Charm of Bulb Growing". Bulbs are "our little brown
friends". There are verses of poetry. At least there are pretty
rhymes. I suspected it had been sent me because I wanted to
acquire the true inwardness of onion growing, that maggot-
infested business. However, it is nice to know that the aconite
has a "green ruffle" and that the iris is "the poor man's orchid"
and that Mother Nature can tend her children far, far better
than we can. By the time, however, that I had turned over a
vast number of pages and was still in a fairyland of flowers, I
had odd misgivings, and on reverting to the title-page read
"1938". I had taken the wrong catalogue off the shelf! Here is
the one that was sent the other day: "1941. Grow more food."
Now I feel at home. This is our age. There is an end section still
devoted to flowers, but it is a case of "Nooks and Corners for
our Little Brown Friends" now. They have been put in their
place. Life is real, life is earnest, and I must buy my seed potatoes
from "the Ross-shire Highlands". But onions—ah, onion sets
are unobtainable. I read up what I should have done in the way
of growing from seed. Whenever the frost rises out of the
ground and the soil dries, I'll be working away over the edge of
the dark. Do I like the prospect? Well, it is not too bad.

And the moon is coming. We saw the slim sickle the other
night as we were walking along the road. So I was told to wish
a wish. At such a moment I never can think of anything to wish.
My mind fumbles and goes vaguely blank. But the gardener
seems to know her own mind and be able to think as quick as
lightning on such an occasion. As my mind groped, it received
from her a hint and a direction, and suddenly I was delighted to

wish silently the early recovery to complete health of our friend in hospital. As we walked along, I turned my head over my shoulder and found a new interest in the new moon. And then came the thought: what would I think of the new moon hereafter if it let us down? When we reached the telephone box and rang up, however, we found that the news was good and is expected to grow with the moon.

March and the Dead Earth

To-day I saw about twenty Highland cattle following a cart of hay across a field. They were drawn out in a line, and with their shaggy dun coats and long horns had a soft wild beauty that held the eye. I have seen them frequently throughout the winter and have often marvelled at their hardihood. Delicately they would nose the snow away and pick up moss or withered grass with fastidious lips. They were never indoors at any time. More than once, late at night, with the small burn a solid sheet of ice, I have heard a rustling beyond the hedge, and on peering through have watched them standing there quietly, eating the twigs of some felled trees. In the frosted moonlight, as they turned their heads towards me, a sense of dumb fellowship could be felt in a strange stillness of endurance.

How truly a product of their environment, how naturally they fit into the native scheme of things! Their milk is rich, and connoisseurs have said of their flesh that it is the sweetest of all. It was not only tragic, it was uneconomic when the Highlands were cleared of the crofters and their hardy cattle together with all the wealth of shieling life, in butter and cheese, in song and story, to make wastes for sheep. In the old economy they knew that the land goes sour under sheep, and so kept heart and sweetness in it with their cattle.

The tufts of shaggy hair hanging down over their eyes may make them look rather ferocious, but they are the gentlest of beasts—except, let it be remembered, when it is the case of a mother and a young calf. Then, as I have heard East Coast people say, "thae highlanders are treacherous". And, in fact, I do know of a man who was lucky enough to get through a fence in time from the charge of one of the timid score that I saw following the hay-cart. But the calf was only two days old and the man had gone between it and its mother—never a wise proceeding in the case of any breed of cattle, or even, for that matter, of (what we deem) the most important mammal of all.

As one who has had to retreat hurriedly from both bull and cow, I have the greater respect for the cow. The bull, I feel, gets a certain blind exaltation out of the glory of the charge, but the cow, the female realist, is solely concerned with the object on hand. Yet I once saw one in two minds during the long second that, I believe, saved my life. Two of us were salmon-fishing, and, walking along a grassy ridge that traversed a meadow by a "dead" bend in the river, we came among a herd of Belted Galloways. We were fortunately some two or three yards apart, and, in the all-important second, I realized not only the astonishing fact that an enraged cow was going to charge us, but also that she did not know which of us to take. I let out a shout and she headed for me, but I leapt down the ridge and threw myself over a providential fence. As she pulled up, her hind hooves, shooting forward, ploughed up the turf. But what I distinctly remember was the roundness of her screwed-up nostrils hissing visible breath. I had hitherto thought that those old-fashioned prints of round nostrils giving issue to jets of steam were a trifle quaint and overdrawn. That we live and learn is a saying doubtless equally old-fashioned. My friend, the true fisherman, made for the river. From a safe distance we saw her nosing her precious offspring.

But these March days are for sheep rather than cattle. Lambs in our quarter are later this year. The month came in on a day of brilliant sun, and as I went with the shepherd to feed some young tups, he told me that he expected to be busy soon, though so far he had heard of no arrivals in the vicinity, and we were walking over sheltered low-ground pasture. The sheep deserted their fenced-off part of the turnip field and came running when they saw him. We got talking about a recent controversy in a farming journal where one disputant maintained against all comers that a sheep not only did not drink but could not drink. We smiled as we looked at the black path they made across the field to the small burn. And in any case, as the shepherd put it, he has had to carry water to them and watched them drink too often in his lifetime for there to be any doubt on the matter.

To these pasture fields, after early stragglers, the peewits have now come in fair-sized flocks, hitting the air with the characteristic slow flap of their rounded wings—whence, I suppose, their name, lapwing (and in French, *vaneur*, from *van*, a fan). When they are really disturbed (as later, in the nesting season), the flap of the wing is very audible, like a drumming sound from taut silk. The other night a number of them must have arrived in the field beside our house, because far into the hours of darkness one of the birds kept crying pitifully. I wondered what was wrong. It was not pain that was in the cry so much as an irreparable sense of loss, of forlorn fear. At first thought, it is easy to say that man attributes to bird or beast his own kind of feeling or emotion. The very little I know on these matters, however, reduces me to uncertain silence. I have met human minds of such great natural sensitivity that it is difficult to avoid belief in powers and kinships of the mind beyond what we can express, or even would express if we could.

Take a little scene I observed some months ago, seeing we have been talking of cattle. A shower was coming up, and I hesitated on the edge of a wood, looking out over a sloping pasture-field whereon cattle of all ages, including a bull, were quietly feeding. As the driving rain reached them from the direction of the wood, heads were raised here and there. Was it going to be much? Faith, it was going to be a heavy shower! The one-year-olds put their heads down and their heels up and started, not so much a serious as a playful gallop, miming acts of butting one another, towards the shelter of the wood. Soon all were affected. One old cow, her tail up, curveted with the youngest, while her deep-hanging udder walloped from side to side. One could not help smiling, because the behaviour was in general so like that of a group of humans who, for some odd reason, laugh and feel gay as, in similar circumstances, they make for shelter. Of course, his important lordship, the bull, approached slowly, bored by such absurd antics over a few drops of rain.

Although there is a fair show of spring flowers, this is the real dead period of the year. It is the in-between season, and was the most trying time of the whole year under the old crofting dis-pensation, when cattle wandered over infield and outfield alike looking in vain for fodder. The feeding stuffs and large supplies of straw and hay, natural to our modern farming methods, were not available then, and, if the harvest had been poor, the beasts over the next month or more would get into a pitiably lean condition. The earth seemed to go dry, a sapless grey turf that yielded to the foot like moss; and even the wind had a darkness in it, despite the brightening days.

All this was brought clearly to mind as, going up a hill road, I passed some croft houses; and then suddenly I was arrested by the almost exotic appearance of three white goats, a mother and two kids, in among whin bushes on a mound on the other side of the burn. Their drooping flanks were sensitive as the flanks of greyhounds, and altogether they had an air of an extreme and yet thoroughbred fragility, emphasized by the sleek whiteness of their thin coats. They were nibbling the outer ends of the prickly green bushes with delicacy but persistence. Then the mother, lifting her head, regarded me over her shoulder with the goat's satyr eyes. The kids, with their short white beards, also half-wondered what I might be. They did not move— except to go on with their eating. It might have been not a Highland valley but the vale of Tempe.

Again the two wild duck were in the pond in the wood, the mallard's head resplendent in burnished green. In the summer time he loses his brilliant colouring and becomes as dusky brown as his mate. They have had rather a charmed life, for they have been stalked more than once and I have seen them missed by a right and left from a shot-gun. The mallard saw me immediately my head appeared among the trees, said a quiet word or two, and out from the reeds sailed his mate, thrusting her neck anxiously. I remained perfectly still. They looked towards me for a time and then, as if released electrically, were up and off. You could see by her flight that she is playing up to him a little. He is the strong guardian and she has a few things of her own to think about. As they are not given to feeding during the day, what was she doing in among the reeds?

Crofter and Collie

On the edge of the moor I met the crofter yesterday with his collie dog. We got talking about deer, for Ben Wyvis was white, and I asked him if the hinds ever invaded his place. "Oh, yes," he said. "Sometimes in the grey of the morning they will be over in the field there, and when they see me they run together and stand still, with their heads up, as if quietly debating which road they would take."

It is a picture that stays in the mind. But then deer have this capacity to arrest the attention vividly. It lies, I think, in the carriage of the head, in that still, questing look, with the sensitive nostrils, the soft eyes, and the pointed ears. Two qualities are suggested in their purest form: grace and freedom. Watch them as they first move away, tentatively, uncertain, with the head not, as it were, leading the body, but thrown back a little, riding the body with a lovely ease.

Every reader will have his own most memorable picture of these natives of the high tops. Mine was acquired in somewhat unusual circumstances. Late on a summer afternoon in one of the long sea-fiords of Argyll I was lying idly in my small boat watching the sun's shadow beginning to climb the mountain that rose some three thousand feet from the water's edge. I had been told that it was impossible to climb the mountain as quickly as the shadow and, on the spur of the moment, decided to try. The shadow easily beat me, for not only was the going difficult at times, with one or two precipices to circumvent, but there were high hills on the other side of the sea-loch. Anyway, a little before midnight, I was sitting against the small cairn on top, when, without any warning, any sound whatsoever, up over the near brow of heather came a herd of stags. They saw me and stopped. I never moved. They were only a few yards away and stood so still so long that they looked as if they had been enchanted. In the eerie spectral light I could see between their legs, under their bellies, through their antlers, mountain ridges against an infinitely remote sky.

It needed something uncanny to go with a picture like that, and it hardly took the hour before it happened. On my way down in the ever-dimming light I came on a sloping table of grey rock. I had to be very careful, because of the treachery of the black shadows, but here I could see quite clearly a dark lump or boss at the end of the sloping table, and all I had to do was to let myself slide carefully down until I got a foot against the boss, when I should be in a position to peer over and see if there was a precipice beneath. The boss was unfortunately a couple of feet beyond my reach while I still held to the upper edge of the table. I let go—and slid right through the boss, which was no more than the overhanging frond of a tall bracken. Before I struck the steep slope some four feet below I had a long time to ponder on man's mortality.

While talking to the crofter, I had been idly following his collie, for more than once I had caught a glimpse of him hunting on his own, though he had always slunk away at first sight of me. Beyond the drystone dyke there was a small bed of rushes, and, even as I watched, the collie stopped, then quicker than hand could nip a live coal off a carpet, the lean muzzle snapped into the rushes and jerked back with a brown hare. The hare never got its head up, though the strong hind legs kicked onward a yard. The collie chewed at its throat. There was a smothered squeal or two, and the beast lay still. I leapt the dyke, but the timid soft brown body was quite dead. I knew the hare well, for I had seen it more than once, and no later than the day before it had provided me with one of the most wonderful instances of protective colouring I have come across. On the ordinary upland lea with the usual few long grey broken grasses and an odd stump of withered thistle over the bare green, I thought I had seen from a little distance the ears of a hare fold back. I came to the wire fence opposite the spot, but manifestly there was nothing there, though the longer I stared the more certain I was I could see the full round dark eye of the hare at about fifteen yards. The only stone I could find was a heavy one, and I pitched it so that it would fall with a thud four or five yards short. As there was no response, I moved off; yet I was not satisfied and came back. I found the eye again with the lids meeting at an acute inner angle. How easy it is to delude oneself, I thought, kicking another and smaller stone out of the grass. I was stooping to pick it up when the hare bolted.

The collie had backed away from me and now stood with the poacher's guilty look on his face, the fur still tufted on his fangs, watching me pick up the hare. He knew that at last I had caught him in the act, and that knowledge now will always be between us.

Pictures in the Air

The morning sun, which had cleared the hill-tops to the south-east, turned the straw of the sheaves on the cart into a glistening gold, a pale gold against the white of the snowy arabesques on the blackthorn.

Then it was that my eyes fell on the old apple-tree in a low corner of the garden. It is really due to be cut down and for some years has been quite neglected. For a moment I just could not believe my eyes, for the tree, though festooned with snow, was laden with golden fruit, with golden pears. It really did take me a second or two to realize that I was looking at a resting flock of yellow hammers, each with its breast to the sun and still as the tree itself.

It was one of the most enchanting pictures I have ever seen. It had that air of the incredible with which great artists sometimes astonish us. It was fantastic; it was real somewhere else.

64

I left them sitting there, and by that unpremeditated act gave to the picture, as I now perceive, a further static quality that time and change can never affect.

The apple-tree and the gold need but the singing to complete them. So here is another snatch of beauty, caught in what man might consider a perfect moment, for we were coming out of a country inn. The ice had been in excellent trim for curling, the air crisp with frost below the sun on this spring day, and as the stones had come singing up the little loch, the skips had chanted their ancient admonitions.

As we drifted out over the doorstep, we heard a bird in full throat, and lifting up our eyes we saw, just over our heads, a robin singing on an outermost twig of an old apple-tree. Now from where I was standing, the bird was caught fair in the horn of the new moon. It was still almost full daylight and the pale wisp of the moon was a fragile loveliness in the blue sky. The bird's beak opened and shut, delicate as the divided husk of an oat.

One man put his hand in his pocket to turn his money over. I followed suit, but found my pocket empty, so I smiled instead, knowing we can't always expect luck of this kind.

In the old days in the Highlands—and no doubt elsewhere—the new moon was looked for and acknowledged in various ways. Though the moon was really the women's planet, and when a woman saw the new moon for the first time she always bowed to it. A girl with bright eyes thus greeting the new moon was a disturbing picture to any lad.

The sun was the men's orb, and they took off their bonnets to it in greeting when they first saw it in the morning. But they lost that happy habit with a few others.

The apple-tree, the singing, and the gold. The sun and the moon. I can hear now in my childhood's ear a young woman's laughing voice, lifted in farewell. She and two others must have been spending a happy evening in our home, for I distinctly hear her cry as they went into the night: "We'll be back with the new moon!"

Bow to the new moon and then use her divinity as a lantern. The Highlander is supposed to have an innate sense of fitness and courtesy. He had, anyway.

And, finally, for a different kind of picture, wherein beauty is heightened for one supreme moment in the suspense of tragedy.

I was not with my friend when this happened, but from the manner in which he related the incident I could see the strong impression that had been left on his mind.

He is a Government Inspector, and was hurrying through a wooded part of the country to an appointment, driving his own car alone and hoping he would not be late, when a roe deer got on to the road in front of him. He slowed up, giving the creature time to take the fence. But whether or not it had been tripped or otherwise frightened when leaping out of the pine forest, it now shied at the wire fence on its left, came back to the road, and shied again at the fence on its right. By this time the car was down to a crawl and my friend was wondering how he was going to get past, for the sensitive beast could be almost everywhere at once. At last, seizing what he thought was a good opportunity, he opened out, but in an instant the roe leaped back on to the road and shot straight ahead.

On the curve of the road in front there was a stone wall as high as the fence, but manifestly the beast was not afraid of this solid obstacle and, making straight for it, cleared it with a lovely grace. He observed the whole action with a supremely heightened intensity, the take-off, the gathering of the legs under the body, and the preparing of the legs to land on the other side, because he knew that on the other side there was a sheer drop into a ravine of some forty feet.

He pulled up at once and hurried to the wall. Down below him, the roe was lying on its back in a foot or more of water, its legs kicking. At last it got its head above the water and tried, struggling, to keep it there, its great soft eyes gleaming upward. After a little time it managed to turn over, its forelegs gathered under it, and there it lay.

My friend was in a hurry. If he were seen taking a roe from a ravine his action might be misconstrued. If the beast were all right, he might only frighten it by attempting to climb down. He decided to leave the issue to the gods of the wild, and drove off.

But the affair haunted him and, business over, he drove back to the bridge, to find that the roe had gone. He was pleased then, for clearly the deeper instinct that had really made him leave the beast alone had been right.

Jibydo

Jibydo is a cock chaffinch who considers it his special duty apparently to treat our house to a regular round of song. "Round" is the only word, for he starts upon the ancient ash-tree by the north-east window, does a carefree swoop to the aged elm beyond the south-west window, and, when he has exhausted his second urgency of song there, takes a double swoop to the old plum-tree in the vegetable garden at the back, where he performs with equal vigour. Then back to the ash again. And so on and on. A merry-go-round, a ring of song, a roundelay. If you are trying to concentrate your thoughts on a problem with too many knots, he sings in your very ear, vibrantly. He either convinces you of the fathomless absurdity of human worldly care or drives you to distraction. Just as a shepherd knows the individual faces of all his sheep, so do I know now the individual songs of all the cock chaffinches. It is the only thing in the whole realm of bird life at which I am really expert. We have christened him Jibydo because of a remarkable trenchancy in his last three notes, thus: ji-*by*-do.

On his first morning this year, I heard the song with curious and mixed feelings. It was not Jibydo, I decided, but his son. The old man's technique was there all right, but not the finish, the splendid assurance. Thus was the son of a MacCrimmon known from the son of a Mackay. But I was wrong. The old pipes had needed tuning. The reeds had been a bit dry. The bag had gone a bit crinkled on him. Now it's the old man himself in full power and full feather. We'll have a few words at each other this year should the heavens not fall.

And I thought they were going to fall on us yesterday. At the foot of the glen there is, as there ought to be, a small town. So if we happen to be out and about we can hear the wail of the siren. The sun was trying to come through the silvery ground mists in the forenoon, when in the distance rose the mournful howl, drooped to a low wail, and rose again; the modern banshee, prophesying the ancient doom and disaster. The glen stood still.

I looked across at the steading and realized, as I had never done before, how very like a modern factory it appeared in its long roofs and compact mathematical layout. I began to apprehend one of the reasons for the destruction of farms.

Work proceeded. The wheels of carts rattled over the stones. Voices of humans and animals were heard in their immemorial way. Then, from deep distance in the haze, came the vibrant sound of a solitary plane. We may be a very ignorant folk, but we won't admit we don't know the sound of the kind of German plane that visits us. Straight towards us it was coming. I heard the cattleman's voice: "I can see him! . . . I've lost him again!" I moved a few yards to get an unobstructed view but visibility was still no more than moderate. The wavering roar was increasing. I stealthily had a look around for the most likely spot whereon to flop. The roar was now constant . . . swerving round, not quite overhead. He was sheering away. Yes, the roar was lessening, it was going from us. It kept on lessening, it faded, it died.

The cart wheels rattled, the sun strengthened; there was a

sudden buzz of planes, an angry buzz, for all the world like bees that found their honey stolen, and off they went. A long time after that, when the incident had been forgotten in the press of work, the all-clear came sounding up the glen.

As the siren faded on the still air, the listening ear caught Jibydo at his roundelay. He really sings very well.

Catching up on Time

Long residence in the country does not seem to have made railway travel and hotel life any more attractive, or committee meetings any more exhilarating. Evidence for the next committee meeting accumulates, and the meeting itself is but a preparation for the meeting that is to follow. Sometimes I find myself standing in a great railway station amid the rivers of people flowing hither and yon with a feeling if not of bewilderment at least of wonder. But one man—an army officer who has seen most of the world—did say to me: "When this show is over I'm going to sit in a croft house in the country and never wander more than three miles from it." I suggested to him that the world was looking forward to such rapid means of transport that at no distant date we should be able to slip across of an evening to New York for a spot of dancing. He would have groaned if he could have been bothered.

A second man, a surgeon, surprised me in another way. I had not seen him for a long time and was spending the night in his city residence. He is a very busy man, for distinction in surgery

71

grows with the years. He asked me something about birds, and I spoke vaguely of a recently published *Handbook* in five volumes. (We are always going to buy or read books in the country but always fall very far short of our intentions.) "I have got those, of course," he said, and added, "I suppose you have *Thorburn*? I managed to pick up the four volumes for £10.' In no time I was surrounded by a select library of bird books, all new to me.

"I find I can take up *Thorburn* at night and have a look at one or two of his bird illustrations and feel refreshed. They positively sing!"

Soon the city was forgotten and burns and rivers flowed through the room, and wooded hillsides sloped from us, and bare uplands and broken tumbled country with warm hidden places at the back of beyond.

And seas, too. For I soon discovered that his secret love in all her lovely shapes is the wader. He mentioned a marvellous book that had recently appeared on the shearwater. Though I had not read it, yet the bird-name was sufficient to evoke an island of the Inner Hebrides over which I had once tramped in the very best company a distance of some eight miles altogether in order to hear the incredible volume of sound a great colony of shear-waters can set up at midnight. Then in the daylight hours to watch them from a boat skimming over the sound between Rum and Eigg, tipping the water with a wing as they bank in flawless grace, is to create a memory that can lighten a city room at any hour. When my host assured me that each of these shearwaters has an individual voice which the writer of the book was able to distinguish, I nodded my agreement at once and told him something of the more homely chaffinch.

But he has gone a step further than the mere reading of bird books, he has engaged simple country quarters to which he can slip away for the week-end, and with binoculars in his pocket hunt his new friends through the seasons and ever-varying activities of the year.

Pain is a dread reality, work a necessity, even committees have doubtless a social function, politics loom ever larger in importance, post-war schemes and communal kitchens command our steady endeavour, and the prosecution of the war overshadows all. True indeed, and we subscribe, and bow down, and dedicate ourselves. But—at the back of the mind there lurks a primeval feeling for the ample and the free, for that which brings us into some harmony with birds and trees and the earth and running water and flowing seas and, perhaps, even with ourselves.

Should this harmony in however momentary or glimmering a form have been experienced by any human being, no materialist will ever afterwards be able to convince him or her of its "illusion"—nor hot-gospeller or ideologist "prove" a theory of hellish compulsions.

Many a man must know the familiar sensation of clapping his hands against his pockets and wondering just what it was he had with him but now has not. I have seen a woman behave similarly, but she is generally able to say at once, "I am sure I had my purse", with the conviction that makes you feel fairly certain she has left it at home. The longest time I have ever known a woman lose her purse is a week, and then she found it again in that extra safe place where she had carefully put it away.

But what the true countryman loses, when he has been absent in cities, is time. And though this is palpably ridiculous, for he may have been having "a good time", yet there persists the feeling that he has lost a section, a certain length, of time. So on his return he sets off to look for it.

.   .   .   .   .

CATCHING UP ON TIME

With the old ploughman, astride one Clydesdale and leading another, I have a few words. It is seedtime. The grain is being sown. One or two of the fields have been limed and look from a distance as if powdered with snow. The teeth of the harrows have combed the brown earth. From the next field comes the sound of the tractor which is finishing off the last bit of ploughing. The work has been going on; it is well forward and the year is opening in light.

In the upper wood the pigeons are massed. They get up with a stormy beating of wings as they see me approach. I do a rapid count of a section and estimate the flock at over five hundred. They are feeding on the new seed and I try to remember the number of grains that a full crop can hold. They are difficult birds to get near, particularly at this time when the trees are so bare. How swiftly they are on the wing; how they swerve and swing away from your unexpected presence. You can almost hear them cry, "Look! he's there!" and then for a moment they hardly know which way to take, like nimble girls surprised in a game.

Rooks behave quite differently. They spread out like a fan or an umbrella and, with the worldling's knowledge, caw both warningly and derisively.

But one of the upland fields has not been ploughed. Its ancient elm midway up the near side stands against the sky bare and austere, a fabulous genealogical tree. Its bark is like an elephant's hide. It waits on time with a supreme patience. A poet might have a vision of it as time itself, especially in the stillness of the grey evening light. An ordinary mortal might go the length of imagining the bird of time as nesting in its boughs.

This field has smooth on-rolling waves like an arrested sea. On one of the crests gulls and peewits are continuously fluttering and squabbling. This happens every year in the period before nesting really begins. Here a peewit is chasing two gulls, and there a gull is diving after a peewit. There may be some method or purpose in these erratic happenings, possibly even some conscience. Manifestly the pursuer is conscious of being in the right and the pursued in the wrong. But nothing is carried to extremes. The method or purpose may be as obscure as the restlessness that keeps them on edge. But they are obviously beginning to formulate rights—or should it be rites? If female birds have a sense of humour, I suspect that they are enjoying themselves just now, delicately and of course decorously.

However, it is all very difficult, for none of them will actually nest here. But this committee has undoubtedly its own terms of reference and that its labours will result in constructive proposals of the most satisfactory kind I need have no doubt. More than that—the proposals will in due course break through their coloured shells into life, a veritable new life, like a miracle. Our human committees can also produce eggs of an ideal and not uncoloured kind, but the trouble with them is that they are so often addled. Perhaps the next great lesson to be learned (or remembered) in sociology is that, despite all our progress in theory and communal effort, the egg is still produced by the individual. The surgeon, anyway, is quite sure of it.

The immediate conclusion I drew, however, from this upland crest was that nesting had not yet started on the high moor and that I should find it deserted. I might have known better. Here the peewits had paired, but clearly they were still in that early delightful state of dalliance which could afford to ignore a mere earth-borne mortal. Not that the male bird did, of course. He dived at me just to show off, and, in the same swoop, dived after his lady love, who performed the dance of evasive action nimbly on the air. Presently she'll change her tune, and dive at me like a tormented termagant.

And here, approaching from three directions, the advance squadrons of gulls. A cock grouse gets up and rocks as he roars at me to go back. From a grassy islet in a lochan two wild duck whirr upward, the duck sticking close by the drake as he wheels.

CATCHING UP ON TIME

How detached from the noisy mass life are these two birds of the wild! One wide sweep and they head into distant and lonely dimensions.

It is time to sit down and have a rest. But what is this? For time that was lost is sitting down also and having a rest. Can it be that when you really find time it stops?

Lambs and Trumpets

We know a gardener, within three miles of Perth, who treats the daffodil as an individual, with results that I shall never forget. There is a glass porch to his country house. Entering it for the first time I was suddenly transfixed—and if I could think of a more dramatic expression I would use it. Bowls of daffodils stood around on a shelf. They were different kinds or varieties of daffodil, I suppose. But the mind at that moment did not think in kinds or varieties; it did not even think in terms of beauty; it was held in the breathless innocence of wonder. One bowl in particular—the first I saw—had flowers uptilted from the ends of their long stems, like a flight of golden butterflies. Yet that man, because he loves his flowers, considered our enormous debt to him fully paid by a simple expression of admiration. Perhaps it is a blessing that accountancy in these matters knows nothing of book-keeping by either single or double entry.

I hear occasionally from a man who is an artist and a yachtsman. I have never met him, but a common interest in the sea and boats somehow started a spasmodic correspondence. From a letter of a month ago, I gathered that the body was not what it had been, for his fond hope was, he said, to live to see his daffodils blow once more. The gardener and myself were talking of him the other evening, glad that his hope had been realized, when we saw our own trumpets lifting, as though he were a friend long known.

How inevitably the thought of our correspondent on his sick couch evoked:

> For oft, when on my couch I lie
> In vacant or in pensive mood,
> They flash upon that inward eye
> Which is the bliss of solitude;
> And then my heart with pleasure fills,
> And dances with the daffodils.

On the whole, March was not a kind month. We had two separate if short snowstorms, and a wind that could hardly tear itself away from the north. Fortunately for our low-lying area here, lambing came between the storms, and on the crofts up on the moor it came after. Although without our weather forecasts these days, the shepherd, who had twenty-four lambs to twelve ewes, was not caught napping by a stormy night and drifting snow. The evening before, in fair weather, he had driven them down to shelter. But what a slow procession was there! For of course the very young lambs got mixed and the ewes went back as often as forward, each trying to nose her own. The shepherd had infinite patience and gentleness, and his two dogs kept off the road altogether. Sometimes you would think the dogs gave a humorous snuffle from lowered heads as they went up the yard of bank to note the absence of progress.

The sheep know the dogs just as well as they know the shepherd. They seem to have a fairly good notion of time, too, for morning and evening they visit the feeding-troughs at the same hour, and if the shepherd is not there they wait a little while and then go away.

Some of the spring flowers were given an unusual brilliance of colouring by the thin sheath of snow over the ground. It was interesting to see glory-of-the-snow with its flowers above the snow. And the blue scillas, too, seemed to have an extra bloom upon them. I suppose one gets these delusions each spring, but I feel certain the scillas with us were never so freshly and deeply blue before. When the sun came out, the yellow crocuses sticking above or partly in the snow (they look larger this year) were all lit up as from inside. The primroses were in such profuse glory that even less than an inch of snow could hardly shake down past them. But they did not mind, and held up their half-veiled faces as if playing a hiding game in which they mustn't move.

There is a wise division of labour in most human occupations, from ploughman, cattleman, and dairywoman on a farm, down to the man and woman on a plot of ground. My job is the heavy digging, and at this season of the year the desire for it comes over me just as mysteriously as marbles did at an earlier age. I have no desire to interfere with flowers at all. They are the music and the dancing rites; they are mood and colour and emotion, aspiration and wonder. I agree that they are all right in their place. But when the spade turns over the black earth— and if the earth is wet it gleams as with sweat—the mind knows that this is the first rite of all, the dark primeval rite, from which cities and civilizations and wars and cultures and things holy and unholy have sprung.

The softened flesh must take it slowly to begin with. But does it? Aches and cramps proclaim the same old folly of tearing at it. But gnarled old trees grow out of that earth as well as primulas. And after a day or two, wisdom comes, and when the back of the work is broken, one goes on in a measured easier rhythm, with pauses for the spinal column, an eye for the inevitable robin, an ear for a singing bird, and nostrils for spring's scents.

After the spade, the rake. After the rake, the rooting out of the home-made line. And last of all, the seed. Leeks, lettuce, carrots, peas, beans, beetroot, radishes—the little flat green packets lie on the palm lightly, while you discuss early potatoes and cabbages with the seedsman, who is bright and busy as a bird. For this indeed is his season. How willingly he advises you —or agrees with you! "You certainly won't be disappointed with them."

You tear off the corner of the packet and the seeds run on to your palm. With a breath you can blow away what will sustain a household for a year. How varied, too, in form and colour are the different seeds—and how constant, each to its own kind!

As they touch the ground, they make little movements in order to lie comfortably, and then you cover them over.

I hardly think I should have mentioned a seedsman and a bird in the same breath; not, anyway, the birds around our place; for they have lost all count of profit and loss and thrown well-regulated custom over the moon. Or, at least, over the star of eve, whose tender beam was shining in the southern sky before a few blackbirds inhabiting some evergreens reached the top of their frenzy the other night. They were beyond song, beyond everything but flight and alarms, and shaking of branches, and emergence therefrom in panic swiftness. All spring's world was their stage, and the subdued lighting was no inconvenience.

In contrast to some oyster-catchers on the edge of Gairloch bay a week or two earlier. A soft balmy day with the sea lapping the sand. They seemed to be asleep in the sun, and when a little wave came and washed the outermost two off their feet, they walked in behind the others, and dozed there until their turn came to be floated again.

I am told that in Eigg and Muck the common guillemots have arrived at their nesting places some weeks earlier than usual. It is normally April to May before they settle upon their ledges on the western outposts, and my correspondent wondered what this might portend. It could hardly be connected with some recent bad weather, because bad weather at this time of year is nothing unusual. So the matter was laid before a native who has had long traffic with the sea in these parts. Looking at my correspondent with a wise smile, he said that it betokened the coming of good summer weather. And now I have to answer this question: "Do you think he really meant it, or was it just Gaelic charm?"

One cautionary note. I refer in these pages to the unwisdom of walking between a field cow and her new calf. I know it is unnecessary for me to tell the ordinary motorist that in his driving between a ewe and her lamb there is far more likely to be fatal consequences—to the lamb. But I should like to draw special attention to some of the remoter Highland roads, and particularly those that go along a slope where sheep may not be on the actual highway itself but where the ewe may be just below it and the lamb a few yards above. The lamb will invariably come charging down to the mother, and on a slantwise course has been known to overtake fatally a carefully driven car. An eye for each side of the road is all that is necessary, and forecasting an animal's action can become a game.

Dancing in the Highlands

The dance between the man and the woman seemed so unusual, even fantastic, for a country dance, that some readers
asked me if I had imagined the whole affair. I hadn't simply
because I was concerned in my novel to give as accurate a picture as I could of the social life of the Highlands about a century
ago.

Doubtless it carried a symbolism that went back to very
ancient times; for as the man sets to his partner he has a small
rod in his hand, called "the druidic wand" or "the magic
wand". As they dance opposite each other, crossing and setting,
changing places, with all the vigour of life, the man brandishes
his wand over his own head and the woman's, and at last hits
the woman with it, whereupon she falls down dead. The expression in dance of his grief then! But he lifts up her left hand,
breathes on its palm, touches it with the wand, and the hand

comes alive. So he treats the other limbs, till they are all alive, each evidence of renewal giving him great joy, which he interprets in the dance. But though the woman's hands and feet are jerking about to the music, her body is still dead. He kneels over it, breathes into the mouth, and touches the heart with the wand. So his woman is returned to complete life and they dance joyously as in the beginning.

In one of his notes to *Carmina Gadelica*, Alexander Carmichael describes the dance as he frequently observed it: "The tune varies," he writes, "with the varying phases of the dance. It is played by a piper or a fiddler, or sung as a 'port-a-bial' mouth tune, by a looker-on, or by the performers themselves. The air is quaint and irregular, and the words are curious and archaic."

He mentions by name several other dances but unfortunately does not describe them, although his mere reference to them is suggestive: "Another dance is called 'cath nan coileach', the combat of the cocks; another 'ruidhleadh nan coileach dubha', reeling of the blackcocks; another 'turraban nan tunnag', waddling of the ducks; another 'cath nan curaidh', contest of the warriors, where a Celtic Saul slays his thousands, and a Celtic David his tens of thousands. Many dances now lost were danced at the St. Michael ball, while those that still remain were danced with much more artistic complexity. The sword-dance was performed in eight sections instead of in four, as now. The Reel of Tulloch was danced in eight figures with side issues, while 'seann triubhas' contained much more acting than it does now. Many beautiful and curious songs, now lost, were sung at these balls."

I must say I would give a lot to see the "reeling of the blackcocks". The "waddling of the ducks" had probably a touch of broad but solemn comedy, interpretive of the domestic scene, but into the reeling of the blackcocks there may have been imported an early-morning concept of love and combat verging on pure phantasy, which must have been exhilarating to behold. One may say as much because some Gaelic verse does exist which describes with an intricate word music the reeling of the blackcocks. Keith Henderson has translated some of it, from which I take four lines:

> Far out yonder
> The Blackcock are dancing
> The Blackcock are reeling
> On the merry hills.

But when it comes to "cath nan curaidh", contest of the warriors, clearly no one short of a Celtic Diaghilev could be trusted to treat the matter to-day!

While browsing through some old books for bits and pieces that might help to give the true economic picture of a period—how economics obsess us!—I chanced on further references to dancing in the Highlands which certainly astonished me. Generally the references are tucked away in "Notes"—as in the case of a long poem called "The Grampians Desolate" (published 1804) by Alexander Campbell. Let us look at what Campbell has to say about it for he does make an effort to give some scope to the picture, thus: "The variety of dances that in former times made part of the amusements or mirthful exercises of the Gael, may be divided into four classes. 1. Dances of one performer. 2. Dances of two. 3. Dances of three or more. 4. Dances of character or dramatic cast."

The solo dance appears to have been largely a character study. For example, a female dancer assumes the character of a *cailleach* or old wife. She dresses "in grotesque stile, having a huge bunch of keys hanging by her apron-string, and a staff to support her, for she affects to be very stiff, and lame of one leg. When the tune strikes up, she appears hardly able to hobble on the floor; by degrees, however, she gets on a bit, and as she begins to warm, she feels new animation, and capers away at a great rate, striking her pockets and making her keys rattle; then affecting great importance as keeper of the good things of the store-room, *ambry*, and dairy. Meanwhile some of the company present join the person who plays the tune, and sing words suitable to the character the dancer assumes—generally some nonsense of a comic cast with which the matron, or Cailleach, seems wonderfully delighted." He names some of the tunes with words, which are played and sung.

If the dancer is male, he also impersonates some character—a droll fellow or a day-labourer or a man with a flaughter-spade who sings as he dances, telling how he got on after his day's work. The poet also names "a kind of wild fantastic dance that requires great strength and agility to go through the various steps and movements, and is danced by one man."

But it is the dancing under heading 4 that is most dramatic and perhaps most interesting to us. He mentions some of obviously ancient lineage, such as "the dance of the he-goats". It is performed by three men, "who reel fantastically, leap, bound, and bleat as he-goats do; and stooping on all fours, they jump alternately over each other, causing by this means much merriment and laughter." But *Damhsa an Chleoca* (the cloak-dance) seems a more social affair. The dancer assumes the character of a young laird returned from his travels abroad, attended by his man-servant. As he comes in he looks around at everyone in wonder "and after rambling through the apartment while the tune is playing, he all at once stops, throws off his mantle, plaid, or cloak, and away his staff, affecting at the same time considerable emotion; his servant, who is by, picks up the cloak and staff and puts on the one, and places the other in his hand, endeavouring at the same time to quiet his master, who seems to be pacified, and foots it away again to the same tune, till he tires, and throws away his mantle and staff again; which his man takes up, and presents them as before; repeating the same several times, till at last the servant recollecting that he has a letter, he pulls it out of his pocket and offers it to his young master, who says he is unable to read, owing to a phlegmon on his posteriors, which marvellously affects his eyesight! and that ****" The four asterisks are not explained, but clearly there was an earthy sense of humour in Lochaber, also capable of translation into the dance.

But the dance that is described most fully is *Crait an Dreathan* (the wren's croft). Perhaps our author found the ludicrous in some of these dances rather attractive. As he puts it: "Notwithstanding the prevalence of the opera in Europe, we still find that national dances retain a place among the pastimes and pleasures of the vulgar, at least, in defiance of refinement, and all its bewitching train of allurements."

The man who works the Wren's Croft has his story to tell. Altogether it was what our author calls "a comic performance", and certainly not concerned with refined allurements. It must have been full of vigour, abrupt at moments, and generally designed to induce gusts of laughter. He comes before his audience and says: "I was formerly the farmer of the Wren's Croft; and if I was, indeed it was very difficult to labour; it was wild, *balky*, stony, *cairney*, and the furrow ill to clear; yet difficult as it was I laboured it. Blow up!"

With the final shout to the piper (or fiddler) he dances through the tune; then stops again and proceeds: "After that there came a great company of soldiers to the country, and they forced me to join them; and they never halted till they brought me to Bothwell-brig. Blow up!"

And he dances again.

He has an adventure with three ladies which requires some asterisks in the English translation (but not in the original Gaelic, also given), after which the piper has to blow up once more.

"When the rest went to the battle, I myself stood in a large thorn-tree I saw over the way; and I drew my broad-sword and I laid about me thus, and so, so. Blow up!"

Having returned home, he shows them the tartan which his own brown Flora made—"and she put the red into the heart of the blue, and the blue into the heart of the green, and a clue of black at the end, and I wear it as you now see. Blow up!"

And if he was satisfied with all that good and well, and if not, he had no more to get. So blow up!

From the almost chance notes of these two writers alone, is it too much to believe that here was a whole art of dancing, which could have evolved into something highly diverse and distinctive, had the social tradition and life behind it been allowed a normal development?

The poet of "The Grampians Desolate", who was an educated man of the landlord class, writes of "our national dances which are daily becoming obsolete, and will, in a very short time, be altogether unknown among the Gael, who are either driven from their possessions, by a change of system, or are changing with the varying hour, and will ere long, most likely cease to be a peculiar people, and sink to rise no more."

But the clearances, which he thus deplores, were merely one aspect of the deeper problem of the break-up by political action of the whole national tradition of a people. Anyway, like the folk-music, the folk-dancing was there; and we do know that other countries, similarly endowed but with a continuing national life and tradition, developed these into the symphonic form and the ballet.

Early Sunlight

What a spell of brightness we have had over the second half of April, of sheer sun-brightness! Usually this spell comes a little later, in May. Indeed, as I have written more than once, the second half of May and all June is normally the most invigorating period in the Highlands, and from headlands that come to mind I can visualize vivid flashing seas.

The wind is usually easterly and cold, but with the coldness that keeps the body in action. And if the body needs a rest, then to drop into a sheltered spot is to know the living sunlight—in an absence of midges and clegs. Up in the round pine wood the red cones are on the larches, and sitting there in the sunny quiet one hears the song of the willow-wren tumbling down among the cones, or the song of the chaffinch keeping to its own eager height, or the sudden amazing volume of the robin, or the mellow distant croodling of the pigeons. An immemorial world, coming from so infinitely remote a past and future that it is here now.

I have a letter from a friend: "I sneaked off yesterday (Sunday) up to the top of the Glen and had a quiet walk among the hills. It was magnificent refreshment after a long spell of war work. I don't think I have ever enjoyed a day so much. Am I getting old? I once took a tough-living lad of eighty-odd years out in my car. 'Man,' he said to me, 'the country gets bonnier every year.'"

When the green humours of youth and the importance of middle age, when ambition and social status and the other odds and ends that worry us have had their innings, when the winnowing process has gone on long enough to cleanse the eyes, why, then one has time to look at the earth, and if one has gathered any sense at all, the earth is seen with a new freshness, which is the old freshness of boyhood, and the marvel of this new freshness makes the country bonnier than ever.

Now my friend is not old. But a deliberate effort is needed to pierce through to that disinterested region which lies waiting. All art, all poetry, has consisted in this process of piercing through. For some mysterious reason we are reluctant to make the effort. And in this mood of reluctance art and literature may be seen as something we can do very well without, as really (if we told the whole truth) a sort of trifling in this deadly world. Yet when we make the effort to pierce through, when we do sneak a Sunday off and set out for the distant glen, what a refreshment of soul and body is there!

What a fool I was to miss this so long! I shall come here often. But do I?

We don't require to go a long distance to meet the earth. As a boy in London I can still see Hampstead Heath and Kew and Richmond Park. In Edinburgh I can lie on my back among the whin bushes of the Blackford Hill. The beauty that surrounds Glasgow—is there a lovelier firth than the Firth of Clyde? But why go on? For out of a few clumps of primula, which can be grown anywhere, one can get at least the colour note, like a note of music.

And in this early sunlight of the year colour does really glow. I mentioned primulas. All over the rockery are certain bunches of them. I imagine I know the names of colours in a broad sort of way, but a lady who visits us at rare times demurred to my facile use of the word maroon, and spoke of some shade or other that is deeper than fuchsia. But I caught her out when she said she was astonished that three bunches within a foot or so of one another should yet be so manifestly different in tone or shade. I said that there was no difference, or rather that the apparent difference was due to the slight variation in angle at which each received the sunlight. "Nonsense!" said the charming lady, and to prove me wrong plucked a primula from one bunch and placed it in another—to find that the shades were alike.

I have a memory of reading somewhere of how Conrad and a literary friend tried to describe the exact colour of some vegetable-top and, after calling in the aid of the French language, had to give it up. I also find it a slight compensation to know that poets like Wordsworth, who started off by using colour words profusely, came in the fullness of their art hardly to use them at all, and yet to body forth the reality of colour more profoundly. They had absorbed the colour right into them, as a few men absorb wisdom. I have heard a wise old man, relating an experience, say, "It was a fine morning". In his mouth it was a line of poetry and all the fine mornings of the world were in it.

What a sheer amount of secret enjoyment is got by city allotment holders these days! I was watching a bunch of them on a pleasant slope in an Edinburgh suburb the other evening. The youngsters had gathered the refuse and set fire to it, and the aromatic columns of smoke were drifting lazily above their rushing, eager figures. The men were busy on the spade. Over a pint of beer they will retail their aches and exaggerate their stiffness. But watch them when the first tiny shoots are coming through. Regard the manner in which they go out "to have a look round". No hurry about it, of course; no obvious pride. But they know that they have produced something here, induced a miraculous creation by the work of their own hands. "Fresh vegetables are so much nicer," say the women. "Every little helps in these times," say the men. Ay! ay!

But something has happened round our own home that gives the gardener the greatest satisfaction. Horses have long necks and a way of eating the tops of tall flowers like lupins which tend to get pushed back ever nearer to the fence. Cows in time will shove their heads through any kind of fence. And there is always the goat. Well, this year the field has been ploughed up, and already the young corn has sent its shimmer of green over the bare earth. Not only will the marauding animals be absent, but there will be green waves for the wind to play with in the summer, and there will be the golden rustle of the autumn that is the best understudy I know to the sound of a forest or to the seething of sea-water down a beach. She is quite jubilant about this, and really I suppose because she may now proceed to do things in a large and hopeful manner. I have a sort of feeling, however, that the goat will probably arrange in his nimble fashion to do a guerrilla raid or two before the year is over, and as she can't throw a stone for toffee (besides, she is always afraid she'll hit the brute) I'll hear about it.

Things are early, as we say, on the farm this year, growth being nearly a month in advance of last. Lambing has been good, too, but the shepherd is already complaining about the persistence of the cold east wind, which tends to dry up the ewes' milk and cause small hacks in their udders. But so far everything seems set fair for a good and fruitful year, though there's no harm in touching wood.

The gulls and rooks have got quite used to the roar of the tractor, and the peewits are not unduly disturbed. I fancy, too, that the greylag geese have made up their minds about aeroplanes as they obviously have about trains. In the last week of March I was travelling between Glasgow and Stirling when a man in the compartment called his wife's attention to a number of large birds scattered over a grassy hollow quite close to the line and inquired if she knew what they were. There must have been over a hundred of them, and they went on feeding unconcernedly as the train thundered by.

The last time I had seen them feeding in such numbers was during the previous spring when the young corn was sprouting on our upland fields, and I thought to myself that this year they would have passed us by before the braird appeared. But I was wrong. Every forenoon in this last week in April I have heard and seen them overhead as they come from the direction of the firth and make up their minds, from their airy observation post, which field to attack. You can see the indecision in their flight. Bombers and fighters are common enough in our northern skies, but plainly the wild geese have decided that they are harmless affairs. Let us hope that from their great height they are able to see farther ahead than we can.

Lambs

The shepherd has a certain number of pedigree Border Leicesters, whose genealogical trees are carefully tended in a large volume, but his real admiration, I think, lies with his Cheviots. One of these had had two lambs that had died, and his immediate intention was to get her to accept one of another ewe's triplets. There are various ways of setting about this, and in the end you can always get the Cheviot to accept the lamb. "But a Border Leicester now, once she has made up her mind not to have the lamb, you can try anything and everything you like, but she will not have it. Do what you like, she remains thrawn."

The Cheviot was standing over her lambs, sniffing them and crying, time about. As we drew near, her anxiety increased. She was not frightened of us, but every now and then she took a little run round, came back, sniffed her silent offspring, and bleated. From solitary confinement in a compartment of the feeding bin, the shepherd lifted out the triplet, and we walked back to the two dead lambs. As he got down on his knees, he shoved the triplet inside his jacket, whence its head poked out every now and again, as he proceeded with the operation of skinning one of the dead lambs.

I thought the ewe was going to leave us now altogether, but her wild circle came back to the starting-point of the other lamb lying so strangely still, so mysteriously unresponsive. Psychologists who have studied the matter say, I understand, that not until its seventh year does a child realize the meaning of death. I felt, from watching her, that this ewe could never realize it—not, in any case, in the sense we do, though there was some instinct brought into play that we have all but lost. Perhaps by going back into our childhood we can get, so to speak, a glimpse of that pure feeling, with its air of fabulous wonder and terror.

The shepherd started between the hind legs and then proceeded as if skinning a rabbit, pulling the forelegs through and stopping short at the head. The lively little fellow was now brought forth from the shelter of the jacket and his head well rubbed with the dead lamb's skin. Next, the skin was thrown over his back, and first one foreleg and then the other introduced into the arm holes of this new jacket. For all the world he was like a small awkward child objecting to being dressed, crying a little but not much, and anxious to be off. But with his knife the shepherd prepared two holes for the hind legs, and into its new trousers the lamb had to go.

"Now," said the shepherd, "let us see how you get on," and he pushed the lamb a yard or so towards the bereaved ewe.

The ewe immediately advanced and, by good luck, first smelt the back and tail (the outside tail, for the lamb now carried two) and not the head. She smelt again. You could almost see her eyebrows gather in incredulity. The smell was perhaps not pure, not all that could be desired, but, by the green grass, it was astonishingly like the smell of her own!

Meanwhile the lamb, weighted by its heavy cut-down overcoat, took a stagger or two in a certain direction, for its emotion was much simpler and more direct than the ewe's. The ewe backed away and had another startled sniff or two. Beyond a small bleat, the lamb bore patiently with this elderly nonsense, and headed again in the one all-important direction, and while the ewe paused to regard us, still with a certain consternation, the lamb joined issue with its desire and gave a small upward prod.

"It's all right now," said the shepherd. He picked up the two dead lambs and we went over to the edge of the field.

In answer to my question as to the likely cause of death, he said it was almost certainly due to a curdling of the milk from the first drink, for there could clearly, from the size of the belly, be no question of starvation. The first drink is a very important one, for the milk is strong. So there by the fence he did a post-mortem, and sure enough the milk in the stomach was curdled into lumps about the size of small loaf sugar. When he sliced them with his knife, they had the close consistency of firm white cheese.

As we went on to feed the pedigree stock in the next field, I had a last look back at the little fellow who couldn't get his overcoat off until to-morrow morning. The foster mother was still having an odd sniff at the superimposed tail, but the lamb did not mind that as he had to make up for his spell of abstin-ence in the feeding-bin, and managed now and then to give even to the superimposed tail a certain gallant waggle.

Border Leicesters are "gutsy brutes". And the goat that wanders about with them (the same that oft-times hath eaten the gardener's rock plants and new roses) puts his feet in the trough. He has a very cavalier way with these high-bred Roman-nosed beauties and uses his horns with a grace and impartiality older than any upstart claims to what after all is a lineage of but yesterday. As one who knew Pan and the satyrs in the glory that was Greece, he is to-day impressed neither by the square lines of beefy commercialism nor efforts at a Roman elegance—whichever way it strikes the eye. If they think they can crowd him out of the trough, they are undeceived in a manner that may feel less playful than it looks. Anyway, it is pointed, and he puts his feet in the trough. But he is not a gutsy brute. He feeds with a certain delicacy, and he even finds time amid the multitude of lowered ravenous heads to lift his own head and out of his long narrow agate eyes give me a look. I cannot truthfully say, however, that I have actually seen an eyelid lower. Possibly his antique humour is too profound. Possibly, too, although he can deal with ewes and scatter their greedy lines when he wants, he finds in the shepherd and myself, armed with staffs, a certain hunnish quality capable of attacking him in the rear. That, however, only makes him the more wary and the more inscrutable. Once, when I chased him from a young and demolished rose-tree, he complimented me on my speed by making rude noises. Nothing will ever defeat the pagan freedom of that eye except death, and even in death it will remain open, holding a little of the ancient mystery and indifference.

Meanwhile the shepherd was drawing my attention to the lambs. They were old enough to attempt a small staccato dance without falling. On the grassy bank near the feeding-troughs they were gathered together, freed from their mothers (now oblivious to everything but food) and cutting all sorts of youthful capers. Races, high jumps, and be daft in a whirling ring, were the principal athletic events. If I had forgotten what it was to be, relatively, about that age, they succeeded in reminding me. Their spirits laughed like daffodils on a windy bank.

But there was one fellow who took no part in the fun. While the ewes were busily eating, he sucked them indiscriminately. He knew they could spare no time to smell him. "There are always one or two like that," said the shepherd. But I watched this fellow closely and saw him get down on his knees in order to command the whole situation more thoroughly. At last the shepherd pulled him off by the tail. There was a froth of milk at the corners of his mouth, his belly was like a drum, and his eyes were glazed. He gave a small belch, went round the bottom of the trough, and, amid that joyous welter of udders, staggered to the nearest one.

Balance of Nature

Birches at Rogie Falls, birches along Loch Maree, birches of
every kind magnificently displayed in the lovely glen that
directs you to Cluanie and Loch Duich; pine woods on northern escarpments, solitary pines by lonely lochs in the heart of
deer forests, pines of striking beauty in the great ravine that
opens out the West on the road to Gairloch; moors barren and
austere stretching vast distances to known mountain peaks, with
green straths hidden in their folds; coast roads playing hide and
seek with the flashing greens and blues of a sea wherein islands
lie at anchor....

Because we cannot visit them now, we are always glad to
meet a man who may happen to wander in. What we want
from him is news, sheer news about fisherman or crofter or
gamekeeper, deer or sheep or wild cat, and an interesting
angling experience is enjoyed in detail.

We had an hour or two recently with a visitor from the
wilds of Caithness and Sutherland who told us some remarkable
experiences of the snow blizzard that swept his northland in the
early part of this year (1941). Inland about seven miles from the
main county road there is a certain small crofting hamlet lying

in a shallow valley with the head-stalker's house at the upper end. There is no shop, and for two months on end they were cut off from all supplies. Twice during that time a visit was made to the letter-box on the high windswept moor, where the snow was not too deep, and though the distance was well under two miles the trip took four hours. But what brought home the desolation to us, who know every corner of that wild glen, was this detail: "From his back doorstep the old head-stalker could count the carcasses of ninety-seven deer strewn over the snow."

A few sheep-farmers were particularly badly hit. He mentioned one case of a man who had lost, it was reckoned, some two-thirds of his flock. Exact detail, however, is very difficult to obtain, because flockmasters are inclined to be reticent about their losses, as though holding themselves in some way to blame.

"I asked so-and-so," said our visitor by way of illustration, "if he had been badly hit. 'I got a nip' was all he answered."

It was the sort of dry understatement that we could appreciate. The real Caithness flavour.

Some of the instances of sheep keeping alive for a long time under the snow were very interesting, and we saluted the old ewe that, when the hay-fence had at last been dug out, was found under the netting eating industriously.

There were incidents, too, not without their humour.

"One day I was walking round that corner just by the bridge when I heard the most extraordinary screams. The blizzard had come on again suddenly and the drift, in fine particles, was so thick that it almost blotted the daylight out. It was really terrific. Well, I looked up and there was a woman standing in the thick of it right on the middle of the road. I went to her and heard her yelling: 'I'm choking! I'm choking!' She was in the centre of the vortex and couldn't move. She had lost the power of motion. Lost her head. She wouldn't move. She was rigid.

I had to put my arm round her and force her off the road to where we could breathe more easily. She was Sassenach; I should say the wife of an officer. Think," remarked our visitor with a merry gleam in his eye, "what she'll say about our barbarous northland when she gets back to the 'home counties'!"

The talk turned naturally to the "balance of nature" and the increase in "vermin". He described a white-hare shoot where the total bag was forty-two, when normally it would have been hundreds. In particular, wild cats and foxes were multiplying so quickly that from a certain district a petition had been sent to Army Headquarters for the return of the gamekeeper because of the destruction of hill lambs.

That the absence of able-bodied keepers and stalkers in the armed forces is going to affect the balance of wild life in the Highlands is already plain. I have seen indications of it on the hill. But even nearer home odd things are happening: rats, for example, have so increased that they are beginning to inhabit rabbit burrows and rob the nests of singing birds that build in banks (though for that matter we have surprised rats climbing thorn trees). Rabbits are now pursued relentlessly for food. As we began to speculate on what would happen to wild life around us if left to its own balancing and the ruthless human food raider, we were forced to what seemed fantastic conclusions.

Our visitor told us quite a dramatic story of how he himself had landed a small salmon, left it exposed while he fished out the remaining dozen or so yards of the pool, then returned—to find the salmon gone. This really worried him as there was no human being within a couple of miles. He had a distinct feeling of the uncanny, and hunted about in a somewhat aimless way for long enough. Even if the salmon had come to life for a few moments, the slope of the ground would merely have taken it farther away from the river. Apart from a hole in a bank some yards away . . . Could it have been an otter? Later in the day he discussed the incident with the nearest crofter, who had a large sheep outrun. The crofter told him that recently he had seen no fewer than four wild cats on a single morning's round. It remains a mystery.

Contrasting Regions

Subtle changes came in the winter brown, and then one day, from a little distance, we wondered if there was an imponderable something added to the larch plantation, an indecision in colour, a faint misting effect. In a day or two there was no doubt about it—the shimmer of green was coming through. More and more it came, until it took the wind in soft tossing waves, and the summer was born.

The birches are following fast. One of the most exquisite pieces of inland scenery in the Highlands lies around the region of Achilty, Scatwell, and Lochluichart. It is a region of not very high mountains, intersecting wooded glens, and the upper waters of the Conon. It is a place where one can get lost in natural beauty, at once impressive and intimate. It is not a set piece, but is both before the eye and round the bend. There is one loch of birches and headlands, of islets and water lilies, which, when I came on it first, gave me the impression of never having been fished by mortal rod. (Actually, of course, it is highly "preserved".)

This is the very home of the birch, and on a sunny April day we rested on last year's dried bracken, through which the delicate wind-flowers or wood anemones were blooming, and looked on a birch caught in its own green fire. In a gorge where the sun's beams came slanting down on trees that hung high over the dark rushing torrent, the newly opened leaves held the light in a glory of translucence that the eye could hardly credit.

If the Scatwell-Achilty region of the Conon River provides one of the loveliest examples of a close gathering of hill and loch and wooded glen, perhaps its most perfect contrast is to be found on the road that runs from Latheron across the county of Caithness to Thurso. Here you have a prairie-like expanse of moor that can be come upon nowhere else in Scotland, not even on the Moor of Rannoch. Though it is not its extent that is the important matter, but its quality in light and texture. Rannoch is sterile and primeval. There are stretches of it that seem to contain the debris emptied out of God's barrows when in the beginning Scotland was made. There is a mood of the weary traveller in which this region can become horrific and overpowering. (I once tramped it all though a long night.)

But on the road to Thurso there is a low suavity of line, a smoothness of texture, a far light-filled perspective that holds the mind to wonder and a pleasant silence. Miles away the Scarabens and Morven rise from the moor in a long mountainous rampart against the sky. They hold the eyes steadily and without distraction. Their outlines are apprehended and dwelt upon. They are the natural "backcloth" in blue or purple to the immense stage of the moor. And a magician attends to the lighting between the flying brightness of the morning and the wine-reds of still evening. Then, as the miles pass, beyond Morven, far into Sutherland, arise the peaks of the Griams and

Ben Hope, and lastly, that enchanted mountain of the granite battlements, Ben Laoghal.

The Thurso River runs through bare flat country, and any guide book would pronounce it dull and uninteresting. There is one broken stretch around the ruins of Castle Dirlot, with potpool and gorge, but it is too short to affect the general character of this treeless river. And perhaps, to tell the truth, one would need to be a salmon-fisher before a liking for its character could be born, and remembered, and not unlovingly dwelt upon. There are days by the Thurso I would not willingly barter for days elsewhere. Many of its pools I know better than men whom I've met oftener. (We have camped on its upper reaches.) The wind blows there, and the sun races across leagues, and when the body is pleasantly tired of the heavy rod, and the wild duck even in the nesting season fly down (keeping to the line of their beloved river) and fly back, you may feel that the earth itself is with you and the world well lost.

I was resting on my back in some such mood the other day, when across the river (down on Beat 2) I saw a boy of about ten and a girl of about eight climbing the short, steep green braes, eagerly collecting some small natural treasures or "bonnie things" and running with them to an agreed rendezvous or "housie". I watched them for an hour. They were utterly absorbed. And I saw, clearly as though it were happening to myself, that it was not a housie they were creating, but memories which they will never forget and which will make that particular bit of the Thurso for ever magical to them.

On the Edge of the Moor

As the old crofter stopped he felt for the grey stone dyke behind him, so that while talking he could also rest. Pushing his cap back, he wiped his forehead with his palm. "Afraid I'm getting done," he said. "I'm not fit for it."

"There's good game in you yet."

"Ah well—I've seen the day! . . . The doctor said a spoonful of whisky would comfort her at night, for she has been poorly lately and not able to do much about the house. I've been west at the Inn Bar. Do you know what they gave me? . . . Half a gill."

I suggested that, in the circumstances, they might at least have made it a whole gill when they were at it. He shook his head. His blue eyes lost their usual liveliness. "Do you know," he said, with the air of one making a strange and desperate confession, "I had not one drop in the house at the New Year itself. Not a drop, and it the New Year! Such a thing has never happened to me before."

I tried to cheer him up by telling him that he was not the only one.

"And the bit tobacco," he said, as if he had hardly heard me, "sure as death, it's getting beyond a poor man to afford it. It is that."

"Poor man?—and you making money as never before off your land and the subsidies!"

But he would not be rallied. He shook his head. "No," he said, "there's no money in it for me. It's all very well on the low land, but up here with us, where the ground is poor, it's a different story. On the good ground they can take eight quarters to the acre, but up here we're lucky if we take two itself. It's not fit for it, and I'm not fit for it, and they shouldn't be asking us to plough it up."

"I suppose labour is the main difficulty?"

"It is. I've been waiting for the tractor. They say there's a better man on it this year, but last year there was a young fellow and he knew little about it, and just scratched the surface. What we did harvest, I kept for the mill, but the mill did not come until the rats had chowed most of it to stibble. But I'm not going to pay, and they can take me to court if they like." The liveliness came back into his eye.

"A pound an acre for the tractor, is it?"

"Twenty-five shillings. And look at the price of seed. Look at the price of grass seed itself. It's beyond what a poor crofter can afford. You have heard of the clearances? The days of the second clearances are among us."

"There are not many left to clear here now."

"No, not many. But I remember when there were seventeen houses along this hill road. You can count the ruins there yourself, though many of them have been cleaned away."

"There would be some good times then?"

"Good times? Och! Och! On a summer's evening I can remember the young men, on that strip of ground over there, at the jumping and the hammer and the stone. There were times then! But where will you find a young man here now? Go over the houses as you like. There's not one. And those of us who are left—look at me!" He smiled. "You'll be thinking I'm grumbling?"

"No, but I can see it's come hard on you to keep the place going. In the old days when a man had his family growing up to help him, it would have been easier."

'Ah, yes, and in ways you would little think of. As you can see, I'm not very soople on my feet. And the nearest shop is nearly three miles away. And I've to walk there every week for our rations. There's no van to the foot of the road now."

I asked him what sort of lambing season he had had, for I knew he depended mostly on his stock. He had a habit of leaning on his stick and shouting at his collie in a way that one might have thought would have been confusing to the dog, but never was.

"It was a hard season. The long spell of north-east wind stopped all growth in the grass. I had to be out and about, helping the ewes at the lambing, more than I can remember for many's the year. The cold wind was bad for them. Very hard it was. But I'm hoping we're through the worst of it now."

"With the opening year things may come a bit better."

"Let us hope so. Though indeed if it wasn't for the kindness of the farmer below me, I couldn't manage at all. But he is kind, I'll say that."

We drifted into talk of "the old days", and he gradually, as we say, came out of himself and told me some amusing stories about strange orgies the tinker clan—now vanished—had at certain seasons of the year, about "old *cailleachs*" who were spae-wives, about *ceilidhs* and "the queer characters who were in it then", about Hallowe'en and New Year and other festivals, until this high edge of the moor came alive in a rich life.

He shook his head, his eyes gleaming now with a memoried intelligence. Out of the old life came some inalienable quality of breeding that could never be done down however physically he might be overcome. He did not have to remember his manners. They were native to him. And whenever the talk allowed him to expand, they flowered naturally.

He hobbled away, but at a few yards stopped and turned round to cry back something interesting. This was a habit of his and it sprang, I think, from some delicacy in the leave-taking that would even inform that with the final assurance of human fellowship.

As I turned towards the mountains I felt it was a shame that the old boy hadn't a drop of whisky for himself. Surely he had arrived at the time of life when he needed it. It was the cordial that had first been distilled out of the moors and the glens. I thought of those who could afford it, who drank it needlessly and endlessly. I thought of the army officer who had spent his leave with us and who told us it could be bought—the very best —at five shillings a bottle in a certain area beyond our shores. And, anyway, that this old man who was so gallantly doing his best to grow grain and meat should have to hesitate over buying an ounce of tobacco seemed more than a bit tough.

Of course, I knew that crofters as a whole were doing fairly well. But that vague way of generalizing an economic position does not help very much when one comes up against the particular instance.

But here was the mistress of the high croft, her basket hanging from the crook of an arm, on her way to the distant shops. We stopped for the usual inquiries.

Yes, things were going well enough, though now getting a bit behindhand with the cold drought that had been in it. But when the rain came it would soon make up. "And at least it's been keeping the weeds down!"

She's a cheerful, pleasant woman, but when I asked after her few sheep, she said with a solemn air, "We lost our best ewe". Then she told me the story.

It was an interesting story to me, because I had heard many of the same kind from this very district. But she gave it detail and life as only the true countrywoman can. They had bought two or three ewes at a sale in the auction mart of the county town. The ewes had come from a distant part of the country. As lambing-time drew near they had become restless and a watch was kept over them. "You have got to watch them then," she said, "because some of them if they get the chance will want to go back to the place where they were born in order to have their lambs there." Crofting fences on high ground are not very good at the best of times, and one ewe had gone.

"And you haven't been able to trace her?"

"No. Something must have happened to her—or someone has taken her in somewhere."

I knew of a ewe that had actually gone back from the Cromarty Firth to the shores of Little Loch Broom on the west coast where she had been born and where she was found again. That ewe may have travelled the road she had been driven, though it was unlikely, for one does not readily conceive of a ewe wandering back through town and village all alone.

A man had once told me the story of a cow he had sold to a stalker beyond the mountains. The cow had been driven in stages along the main road—a circuitous route but easy. A few nights after the sale, his wife nudged him awake. "That's Rosie the cow come home again," said his wife. "Don't talk nonsense and go to sleep—wakening me like this!" said he. "I know her moo," said his wife. In the end she got him wakened properly, and out he had to go in the grey of the morning. There was Rosie, and she bellowed to him in greeting. Later it was proved beyond doubt that Rosie had taken the short cut by mountains and through glens she had never seen before, and manifestly had not been troubled by indecision on the way.

As I came among broken ground, with grey salley bushes and the whin in bloom, I was suddenly among a world where everything was immemorially at home. A lark, with widespread tail and fluttering wings, hovered a yard or two above the ground, leading me away; peewits called and beat the air with vibrant wings; a pair of partridges—I was glad to see them—arose with a whirr; but I could not spot their crouching young; a baby rabbit cocked its head with a foolish air of surprise.

And suddenly I had the illusion that I knew not only what was deep in the mind of the ewe and the cow, but what remained hidden, with forsaken and sad fondness, in the mind of the crofter.

Wells and Wishes

"Did you ever wish at the Clootie Well?" I asked her.

"Yes."

"What did you wish for?"

She laughed. "I won't tell you. I have never told a living soul."

"Why? Did it come true?"

"Yes." She flushed and laughed again. Her brown eyes were so bright that she withdrew them restlessly lest they give some glimmer of her secret away. Her mirth sank inward in delicious embarrassment.

The larches were also fresh and vivid on the path down to the Wishing Well; and the grass was starred with wood anemones. The first violets were here, too, and the red bells of the blaeberry. The waters of the Beauly Firth lay visible throughout their course like a wide river. Beyond the firth were the Black Isle, Ben Wyvis, and all the hills of Ross. On the left, the Great Glen went marching south, while northward Sutherland and Caithness faded into blue distance.

It was the first Sunday of May, the first of summer, and from the high ground of Culloden this vast expanse of the Highland world, with its capital set in its midst, was indeed a noble prospect.

The description recalls Dr. Johnson. He did not think very much of native Highland culture (unless informed by his Graeco-Romanism) and was positive—he was always so positive—that no manuscript existed in the native tongue that was over a hundred years old. That he was immensely wrong is no matter, but on this clean, sweet May morning how confirmed his positiveness would have been at sight of "pagans" in their thousands visiting an ancient well to wish a secret wish! And on the Lord's Day, too, in what misguided Gaelic rhetoricians called the God-fearing Highlands. Even Boswell might have wilted (though we may reasonably doubt it).

It is difficult in this sunlight to be solemn, even to have a sly dig at the learned doctor, for in the general excitement there is an undercurrent of happy fellowship. One wonders what some of them here would say if his gargantuan figure suddenly appeared. There is a point of view which comes not from learning but from the well-springs of life. The girl with the brown eyes would certainly have a vivid reflex. "O Gyad!" and she would run off, lest something of the scrofulous corpulence touch her. The doctor would get his own back in the intellectual realm and she would not grudge him any triumph there.

For this is the morning of the folk, not of learned doctors or of puritan divines. Age or appearance has nothing much to do with it if *the spirit* be right, though it is essentially a festival of youth, for the year is at the spring. Far back into prehistory, the folk had come to this well. Over the rise of the hill are the Standing Stones of Clava, stone circles and burial cairns implying a way of life, with religious and burial rites, we can but dimly guess at.

There is still a saying in the Gaelic north: *Tha e fo dhrùidheachd*, which literally means: "He is under druidism"—that is, he is bewitched; and another: *Tha e ri drùidheachd*—"He is into druidism"—meaning that he is talking like a lewd pagan, for the time came when druidism was lewdness to Christian thought. What was in nature was the enemy of the Christian who considered himself born in sin.

"What exactly did you do?" I asked her.

"Well, I just put my silver coin in the well and drank and wished my wish. And then I tied my clootie to a tree."

"Why the clootie?"

"Oh, well!" She laughed. Why does anyone? asked her eyes. What a silly question! "But there's one thing," she added, "you must wear something new."

"What did you wear?"

"Ah—let me see." Her eyes veiled and flashed. "A new pair of stockings." And she danced around with such enigmatic glee that I knew it wasn't stockings.

"And what did you do then?"

"Oh, do you know," she said, suddenly confidential," we played football. Wasn't it awful?" The thought of this awfulness bubbled up as if she had been touched with *drùidheachd*.

"And then we went down through the woods. What lovely woods! Oh, it was lovely there. And we came to a cave. Oh!"

"And weren't you ashamed of yourself, it being the Sabbath day?"

"I was. I am. But it was lovely!"

A week later I was taking a visitor to see Culloden battle-field, which is on the moor crest between the Wishing Well and the Clava Stones. He expressed a desire to see the well. So we went down the path, now utterly deserted, yet in some odd way not lonely. "You can see the folk have passed this way," my companion said, looking at the grass that had paled under many feet. Vendors of ice-cream and soft drinks had been here; oranges had been sucked and paper bags burst but every trace of all that had vanished. The path was soft underfoot; in the air was a tang of scent, invigorating but so elusive that it took a little time to trace it to the delicate green plumes of the larches.

The larches were on the right of the path: on the left was a plantation of young pines guarded by one sentinel notice proclaiming the danger of fire to this STATE FOREST.

My companion regarded the notice in silence. Then he saw a tiny strip of blue linen or silken material tied to the top-knot of a small pine. It was like a fairy's pennant. "What's that?"

"A clootie," I explained, "a rag of her clothing which a young woman, wishing a secret wish, tied there."

Teaching the Young

The eye has no conscience. When it observes something in the world of nature in which it is interested it wipes the mind clean of the papers on the desk before the window, of the work that has to be done. In a moment like an eager boy of an earlier world it takes the mind in tow and off they go. At the back of the mind, the mind knows well that this is reprehensible conduct. But deep down in the mind, the mind, knowing this, brings a gleam to the eye. For it has a much older knowledge than is dreamed of in the philosophies it has so patiently reared.

This morning the eye picked up some chaffinches pecking about the gravel. It mightn't have paid any attention to them were it not for the earnest conduct of a cock who was showing his lady love how to find seeds for herself among the gravel. Well, said the mind, isn't he an old fool now! For when it comes in earnest to finding seeds or other food or anything to do with keeping life going, she could give him points and not miss them. Yet here she was, playing up to his vanity. Both of them really ought to have more sense! So the eye had a real

look at this normal play-acting and found that it wasn't his lady
love but his daughter, very becoming in delicate yellowish-
green pastel shades, a trifle doltish on her feet and stupid in her
understanding, yet with that air about her of being at court, the
whole court of the new world, and not altogether impressed by
the fussy practical way in which her parent troubled about those
quite uninteresting seeds in the gravel. Once or twice she did
peck one but without conviction. Perhaps she might have
trifled with scented peach-fruit of exotic flavour. Romantically
she held her head up and looked far away. A cock sparrow
landed near her, a squat worldling, flattened in sin. He made to
peck her out of his important way. She evolved a somewhat
ungainly retreat and then paused to regard the impertinent
fellow more directly, but the sparrow, bored by the very sight
of such family ties, flew away. The family were six in all and the
eye lived with them for quite a time.

Earlier in the year there had been a discovery that delighted
the gardener. To the lane above the farm come a few willow-
warblers every season. When we lived in cities spring came
with the leaves to the trees down long suburban avenues or in
the city parks. To folk in the country, the promise of summer
arrives with the cuckoo or with the swallows. But for us in the
country now, the song of the willow-warbler is the true opening theme. When its round notes fall through the branches, like
coloured bubbles of pleasant thought, our minds are not only
assured of the summer that is coming, but of all the summers
that have been. For it is a reflective, not an urgent, song.

From the grassy bank beneath the hedge a small brown bird
flew out. Fifteen yards on and there was the nest, partly domed,
lined with white feathers, and full of eggs—six, no less, their
white speckled with soft rust. It was the first of the kind the
gardener had ever seen, and it was amusing to observe her torn
between the desire to have an egg on her palm and fear lest as a

consequence something untoward might happen to nest and bird.

It was more interesting after that to watch the ways of the willow-warbler, hunting insects among the leafy tree-tops and sometimes catching them on the wing. A quick, elusive brown morsel, singing its sunny song every two or three minutes.

After an absence of several days, we went up the lane again, the gardener wondering if the nest was still all right, when out from the bank tumbled the poor mother bird, and ran along the ground before our feet, staggering, wings trailing. "Ah, poor bird, it's hurt!" she cried, and followed it to the undergrowth by the small burn where it disappeared. She was deeply distressed and turned back to the nest. It was full of the very young. What a shame! The poor bird! And then she saw me laughing.

Later, up on the moor, we came across a marked demonstration of this fearless care of the mother for her young. We walked into a covey of grouse. The old cock was the first to get up and clear off, shouting for all he was worth. We were on a slight slope and for a few seconds it really seemed as if the slope itself were catapulting balls of feathers into the air. You expected them to hit the opposing slope with a thud. Our attention, however, was immediately distracted by the hen. She was only a few paces from our feet, running round in half-circles, a wing trailing, her head down, really in a very bad way. She fell sideways twice. It was so fascinating to watch her that we forgot all about the others. Once a man has pursued game birds, the thought of their possible destruction at such a moment leaps to his mind. I involuntarily estimated the chances of this being done at that moment. Then the hen got up and flew swiftly away, and we still wonder whether the youngsters cleared the opposite crest!

On the moor track to the mountains many an interesting incident occurs amongst bird life as the young are being reared, but this last month a very unexpected thing happened to Old Granny the cat nearer home. Like the other cats, she is not our cat; she merely lives here in an outhouse. Most of her life she lived in the byre over at the steading, where her reputation as a hunter stood very high; but last winter she elected to retire. Her front teeth had got worn away in the chase and sometimes her tongue hangs in the hollow where they used to be, so that in her meditative moments, which are many, she looks like a pantomime cat, a very solemn pantomime cat, that in her profounder abstractions reconstructs the facial movements necessary for saying *meow* without actually saying it. Well, she retired to us, that is, to the gardener, who called her "poor Granny" in gentle tones as she presented the saucer. Granny, however, showed little inclination for milk, and even less for porridge and milk. She preferred meat nicely cut up or even a little fish. Now the meat ration is rigidly enforced even in farming territory, and I think it is very hard on a fellow when the occasional precious morsel on his plate is watched by a pair of eyes that wonder if anything will be left over. It could be argued, no doubt, that Granny by killing an astronomical number of rats has in her time done more for food production in our country than many human beings, and that she is fully entitled to an old-age pension. But that surely is a matter for impersonal argument only.

However, one day a rabbit ate a round score of my early cabbage, and as he would duly eat all the rest I lay in wait for him and shot him. I had got out of the way of shooting and soothed my feelings by grimly reflecting that here at least was a feed for Granny. But when I skinned the brute I found a cancerous growth on its body.

Some time thereafter Granny appeared with a growth on her body. That rather alarmed me for I dislike the idea of disease about the place. As the growth grew, I offered to shoot her; but the gardener said "No" in a certain voice. I scoffed, for Granny's interest in the cat population was known to have ceased years ago.

I drowned two of the kittens and left one, and the way that old cat renewed her youth and brought up her offspring was astonishing enough, I must admit. For she was not young and temperamental, but calm and strict; she was fond, but not foolish; she removed her tail when it was pounced upon and bitten too much; in particular, she patiently but thoroughly instructed her daughter in cleanly habits.

These things I could not help observing at a distance, and what I did not observe I was told. Then one day I heard my name being shouted. But it was not a falling bomb: it was Granny with a young rat and the rat was alive. With the rat in her mouth Granny growled fiercely at us, then turned to her kitten at the door of the coal shed. The kitten was stiff with excitement; the black beads of its eyes glittered.

"Leave them alone," I said impatiently.

But presently I was recalled by a scream. The young rat had got into the kitchen. I pass over the hunting scene that followed. The final shot consisted of Granny, with more detached complacency than any pantomime cat has yet achieved, watching her daughter toss a dead rat and perform a four-footed dance, tail up, of remarkable agility. From scenes like these, I suppose, we may hope that the oatmeal ration will benefit.

But I am not going to begin writing about these cats. It is too tragic a subject altogether. Yesterday morning when I went round by the back premises for a scythe, here was Granny's progeny with back up, tail elevated, spitting fire. The sight of the ginger morsel thus roused might have drawn a laugh, did not the eye immediately search out the cause, which was an entirely new cat, all black, with mesmeric greeny-blue eyes. I had never before seen such eyes in a cat. They were more arresting than the burning eyes you see at night when you can't see the beast they belong to. It seemed to have no sense of the kitten's presence and no fear of me, and the *meow* that came from it had a strange startling quality, startling as it were to the cat itself, as if it still could not credit the extraordinary thing that had happened to it. The brute was fey.

I saw in a moment that it had been in a trap, that its right foreleg was pulped, and that it was as thin as a rake.

I swept the kitten aside, went into the kitchen, and came back with some liquid nourishment. It began to lap it up ravenously.

Late last night the gardener found it in the rain by the kitchen window. It could not stand. She carried it into a shed and made it a comfortable bed. She wondered if there was anything more she could do for it by way of administering a restorative cordial. Knowing what she meant I told her grimly that though we could buy lashings of Sassenach beer we could not buy a bottle of Highland whisky any more.

The cat died this morning. I have already buried two, discovered in much the same condition. This rabbit-trapping is a murderous business.

Grouse Chicks

On the moor in the afternoon I flushed two grouse, cock and hen, almost from my feet. As the wind was behind me, they must have been aware of my coming a long way off and therefore it was obvious they had a special interest in lying close. But gaze as I would on the ground all around me, I could find no trace of nest or eggs or other treasure. And it wasn't as if anything could lie concealed, for the heather had been burnt the previous year and the peaty soil could be seen between the old short stalks and the flat little bits of new heather. I was going to give it up and step on, when right under my nose I saw two dark beads in a yellowish morsel and recognized a very small chick. Now that the eye held it, it seemed, of course, plain enough. How close it lay, how attractive its colouring and form! What instinct had made so young and delicate a thing crouch in such absolute stillness while its parents, on whom it depended, had flown away? The father had not even said as many words as he usually does when disturbed. I looked all around but did not see any more young ones. Could it be an only chick? Slowly I put my hand out towards it. Then it knew I saw it and, breaking into life, set up a thin piping as it ran away. At once three more thin pipings around my feet and three little bodies running away, all in the direction the parent birds had flown. But even a family of four is not a very big family, though it was hardly likely that any others would have elected still to lie close. But yes, here was one more, at about four feet. It was really difficult to see, for it had wedged itself between a heather stalk and two inches of a slope and was slightly tilted over. Feeling I had disturbed them long enough, I walked on.

Off for a Few Days

Once more a holiday snatches at some of its youthful vigour and irresponsibility. I see how of old it was a direct escape—an escape from school, from the office desk, from the workshop, from the compulsion and monotony of toil. The eager young mind was "clearing out", getting back into an ampler world. The new kind of critic may talk about escapism as much as he likes. The new kind of politician may tell of the higher need for identifying oneself with the Party, for submerging one's individuality in a unity of the State. To pot with all that. I'm off! I'm away! Cheers!

Away even from the big-business farmers who have been complaining that the year is a full month behind. The year is always doing something to the farmers, who have their unending trials and troubles, poor fellows. The year is now rapidly overtaking itself and we may have an excellent harvest, but how can anyone—especially a farmer—be sure of such a happy outcome? No, no, it has really been hard, dry, cold, east-windy weather with no growth in the ground. Milk poor and scarce and no feeding stuffs. It's a marvel to see the calves dancing about as they are. That a cherry-tree can have the face to cover itself with milk-white blossom five weeks later than last year just shows it has no conscience. And the birches on the North road—there they were coming into belated leafage with all the freshness and innocence that they normally affect, like folk who have overslept a little and awaken, not with hurry and misgiving, but with pleasant wonder at having had such an unusually good snooze.

But birches, as they give a delicate green yawn, have always been a trifle shameless, more than a little wanton. Of course, they know they can afford to be, they are so beautiful. It makes a big difference to all concerned (with the possible exception of the admirable dowagers who run committees) when you're beautiful. And then, that early morning stretching of eager fingertips to the sky, that exquisite translucency of the leaf, that transparency of the diaphanous robe, that catching up of the whole tree in green light! The old Greeks had a nymph in each tree, a hamadryad. But they were capable of recognizing a lovely thing when they saw it. Moreover, when they called it up they did not put it on a committee or in a squad, they put it in a work of art—not an official academy picture but any familiar household utensil like a vase or an urn. After two or three thousand years, Keats still found something to say about one of those urns.

> What leaf-fring'd legend haunts about thy shape
> Of deities or mortals, or of both . . .

And of course he heard the pipes that play

> Not to the sensual ear, but, more endear'd,
> Pipe to the spirit ditties of no tone.

There's a feeling about that to quote Keats is the literary form of escapism if not of sentimentalism twopence-coloured. To pot with that too! The ditties of no tone are at least a change from the literary rats that crawl down area steps to the brothels before the invisible church. We are due some fresh air some time. And clear shapes in the sun. And a few leaf-fringed legends if we are lucky enough to find them. Not all bees are in the bonnet. There are still a few real ones that gather real honey from real flowers. They sting you quite painfully if you don't know how to handle them, which is fair enough. It's even a fair prophecy that two or three thousand years after this someone will have something equally unique to say about what Keats had to say about the Grecian urn. For what they say is the flower and the leaf of our wintry tree, the ancient yggdrasil.

We stopped at an ancient well and poured a small libation to the old gods and ourselves. We were well on our journey now, and when at last we came to the end of it, there stood kindness herself ready to shake our hands.

Kindness varies much in quality and in degree, in expression and lack of expression. There is a kindness that is kind because it is the right thing to be and you are the right person to receive a portion. There is the charming kindness that oils the social wheels. There is the kindness of well-ordered hospitality, and the kindness that knows it is not wasted. To say that all the kindnesses of the head are calculated is not to detract from their admirable value.

There is, however, another kindness, and it knows neither limitation nor condition, because it comes from the heart with the warmth of the blood. It is a fire you can sit around on a wintry night. The young birch in the warmth of the sun has nothing "on" it; certainly the birch is a trifle thinly clad and cold, and just a little touched up with airs and graces, when you come to think of it. Real kindness has no such graces, because in itself it *is* grace.

It includes even the cow, for the cow belongs to the household and is not in business. An old-fashioned cow, with very intelligent eyes. She comes to the dyke of the park and says "Moo!" when she wants a drink. Her milk aspires to the condition of cream. Cream, real cream, rich and thick and bubbly. Porridge with such cream is a food. When you pour a lashing of it over the finely textured porridge, the porridge breaks up and floats amid the cream like an archipelago. I recommend all persons who like porridge to take it in this way.

The hens, like the ducks, are also members of the family. They have never heard of incubators and electric light, and when they lay an egg they are not ashamed to tell the world. And with reason, for out of the egg comes a curdly white that wobbles on the spoon. I have heard a man say after a time: "I'm ashamed to look a hen in the face". But these hens go on looking into your face with naive expectation.

There are two important things about fish: the kind of fish and its freshness. I cannot tell what kind of fish is the lemon sole I have gotten recently in city restaurants. It tasted like an interesting cross between an undergrown watery rock cod and a dogfish, toughened slightly by long exposure to our atmosphere; that is, when it didn't carry that more or less faint oversmell to remind us of our sad mortality. Now a real lemon sole, fresh out of the sea, with snowy texture . . .

We admired our host's garden. He is truly a remarkable man with his hands. But when we appear, he leaves the garden alone and places himself, his knowledge, and his tackle at our disposal. He never asks us to work in his garden. He merely arranges an excursion up one or other of two glens. This year the primroses as well as the birches were late. Every bank, each nook and cranny, were starred. You would think they had decided to make up for all the man-made ugliness in the world. Peewits, curlews, warblers, finches, wrens, and robins call and sing here exactly as they did in our childhood; i.e. in a manner subtly different from that which we have encountered else-where. We also saw two salmon in a pool. But I refrain from adventuring on a description of new-run salmon amid the crisp greenery of new-born salad.

And so we forget all about the war? On the contrary, planes fly over every day. Our hostess, who has a son in the Air Force, knows them by their engine sounds. Her happiness would be complete if only they would land in the cow's park and come in and have tea. She loves them all and calls them "My boys".

It was almost as strange as reading Keats. But glory be to the God of this still fair earth, we throve on it.

Dawn at Sea

Now and then a sudden craving comes for the sea, for the movement and tumult that the land has eternally frozen into valley troughs and mountain crests. From the sea one can come back to the quiet land as a child to its mother, but the old primitive father holds sway over the sea. "The sea is in his blood"—but how seldom do folk say the same of the land!

So I reached the northern shore of the Moray Firth and at 4 a.m., as I was finishing a drop of hastily warmed milk, the skipper's tap came on the window. I blew out the paraffin lamp and joined him outside.

"I thought I'd take a walk past—in case you slept in!" There was no hurry in the voice nor in the still realm of moonlight and we walked over the tree-shadows and down by the stream. The cottages were asleep like sheep in a park. A small wind from the north brought a frost-chill to the air. The wind would go round with the sun. It was going to be a lovely morning.

A masthead light was coming in over the bar. The skipper named the boat. She had gone out at four o'clock the previous afternoon and had been fishing all night. As she came alongside we saw some open boxes full of haddock ready to be slung ashore. The haddock were gutted, and there were ten boxes altogether, each weighing six stone. Not much was said by way of greeting. A quiet word or two. A tidy forty-foot boat she was, all electrically lit, and the young skipper stood in his long white rubber boots by the wheelhouse.

And here is our own boat of about the same size and build, but with a Diesel instead of a Kelvin engine. The two lads who make up the crew are already on board, and I climb down the single rope, searching with my toes for crannies in the high stone wall, and land on the grey coils of the seine-net rope. In the engine-room aft there is the hiss of a blow-lamp, and presently the engine is running. We hang on to a mooring and the boat's head swings slowly round. Then the warp falls back against the harbour wall—for each boat has its own station— and we go ahead. The pulse of the sea meets us at the end of the cement quay and we stand straight out.

This is the moment one thinks about on land, this first lifting movement under the feet. The sea itself lifts to the horizon in an expansiveness that lifts the spirit with it. Eyes grow clear-sighted and muscles ready and prepared to be lively. The skipper ushers me into the slim wheelhouse where there is no room for two, lowers a glass panel, and stands outside by the opening. The compass is overhead in the roof. The throttle is no slim affair such as I had had on my own small motor cruiser but a tall T-shaped iron key thick as a forefinger. It takes eight or nine half-turns to reduce full speed to dead slow, so there is considerable flexibility. You can steer with one hand and put her out of and into gear with the other, for the gear lever is also a wheel and turns forward or backward with neutral midway. It is only a 26 h.p. engine but it is tough and can be left alone. Indeed no attention was paid to it, nor did it stop, from the moment we left harbour until we tied up over eight hours later.

These mechanical details I find refreshingly interesting. And in truth you cannot afford to neglect the smallest thing on a boat at sea. Moreover I was in the mood to ask questions, for war had not yet broken out, and the economic position of our fishing boats was growing steadily more desperate. The skipper, who was a very old friend, had a lot to say about this, even if I did not then realize how truly prophetic were his final words: "It will take a war to bring back prices."

We discussed every aspect of the problem as we made for the fishing ground. Than the boat we were on, it was difficult to conceive any kind of fishing craft that could be run more economically. The average daily fuel cost was round about ten shillings. She could carry a drift of up to fifty herring nets. True, her range of operations was restricted compared with that of the herring drifter, but then her running expenses were not a tenth of those of the larger vessel. Moreover, she was particularly suited for creek fishing and might revitalize the half-derelict little harbours along our coasts if reasonable prices and intelligent fishing regulations gave her half a chance.

It went deeper than that, too, for local knowledge, expensively gained, is required for inshore or coastal fishing. In the course of generations, as I well knew, the best spots for line-fishing came to be known very exactly, but in the recent change-over to the seine net everything was strange again, from the gear to the sea-bottom. Some of the best line-fishing spots for large haddock cannot be touched with the seine net, for the ground is "hard" and on it a net may not only tear but become a total loss—not to speak of chafed or broken ropes. And the net and its coils of rope are expensive—with prices going up. "Last year I paid 38s. 6d. for a single coil of rope, but this year it's £3." And the coils of rope attached to a busy net do not last many months.

Thus as we gave ourselves to the sea we found our footing among the unstable and desperate elements which have to do with cash and markets, not with the sea and storm and hardly won knowledge and courage and endurance. It was a good kind of talk in this unearthly twilight; it made sure of the body; and

I could already see it was going to be a remarkable dawn. The sea had a long easy rhythm, the sort of slow underswing that would send the first rays along the water in ever-vanishing cartwheels of spangled light. I was looking forward to this and cast an eye now and then towards the far horizon where the red rim of the great ball would come up behind the ocean. Some ghostly gulls were flying around but mostly they were riding the water, for now under the skipper's direction I was putting her about for the first drag.

And what an exact science it is, this business of dragging a seine net along a mathematically plotted strip of the sea's floor. From trial and error, the skipper had come to know the bottom twenty or more fathoms below him as an angler comes to know the bottom of a pool. Three miles out at sea he could with confidence say that if he were a fathom more inshore his net would stick. This may seem incredible to landsmen, but here is what exactly happened later on that morning. I was at the wheel and we were paying out the port rope when the skipper said casually: "There's a smooth boss of rock down there, for sometimes our rope gets it and is dragged under. But we keep going ahead until there's a *twang*!—and up it comes again. We're very near it now." Within three seconds the rope was gripped as by a great hand from below. I waited with more tension than was in the rope, then *twang*! and up it came to the normal angle. Yet now in this grey light before the dawn I could not have said whether we were two miles offshore or three—except that I knew it would be wise to be at least three or the Fishery cruiser might be down on us for inshore poaching.

"See Clyth Lighthouse yonder on the rock? See Bruan Kirk farther in against the sky? . . . Well, when you get the kirk just opening on the lighthouse, you're on the three-mile limit."

And then he started putting me through the science of the "meases"—an old local word for the plotting of two shore lines that meet in the boat, with as wide an angle between as possible. In this way a position is precisely fixed, and many narrow runs dragged by the seine net are named after some particular landmark in the meases, much as pools on a river are named from some prominent physical feature on their banks. The whole known landscape took on an added interest. Three miles out, too, all was on a smaller scale, map-like, so that the eye covered a long foot-journey in a short glance. The familiar became a little strange, strange as the toy cottages and the little chequered fields. The Rock of Ben-a-chielt was a knob on the horizon. The second park dyke east of the Latheron Burn was a straight line. When the straight line ran into the knob you had to find your second line among the hills that were opening west of the Scarabens. Mountain, plateau, glimpse of grey road, a house, a peat stack, headland, stream, hollow—all were pressed into service, while the engine never stopped and the wheel turned to port or starboard.

Moreover, over the more open ground the meases of each drag were mentally noted, so that, in the event of success, they could be at once repeated.

The skipper now held the flag—or "dan"—ready to drop it overboard. It was a thin stick, longer slightly than himself, corked and weighted to keep upright, with a worn Union Jack at its peak and a herring buoy to float beside it. When he let it go I kept the boat going full speed on the given course. Swiftly the rope on the starboard side uncoiled, while one of the lads stood by ready to check it should it loop in going over.

As there are some 400 to 500 fathoms of rope attached to each end of the net, we travelled a considerable distance before the skipper made me alter course to about right angles, and shortly thereafter to throttle down to slow, for now the net was about to go out. The glass and the iron balls that acted as floats to the weighted net in order to keep it upright on the bottom hit the clearing board astern and bounded overboard like balls in a rattling game.

Soon the net was out, and when we had run a short way on the same course, the coils of rope on the port side now whisking out, the skipper told me to bring her round on the flag. But, stare as I would, I could not pick up the dan, until its slim line was pointed out against the sky at a distance, in that moment of illusion, that seemed fully ten miles!

By the time we had fetched the flag the port coil of rope was out, and now with the end of each coil made fast to its winch we went full speed ahead until the two ropes gradually came together as the wings of the net, like a moving fence along the bottom, slowly closed in, directing the fish into the long bag behind. After about twenty-five minutes the winches began to haul in, strongly checking our speed, and by a clever piece of mechanism the ropes were coiled on deck and left ready for the next drag.

At long last the floats of the net appeared, and my suspense as to our catch could be relieved. "Not much," said the skipper, for a heavy catch floats the net early to the surface. But it was not so fruitless as all that, for when the bag was untied a full box of prime haddock slithered on the deck. But I had not much time to look at them, for we were off again, leaving the skipper and one of the crew to gut the fish and grade them into boxes.

Immediately the winches had started, the gulls had left the sea, for they are the scavengers of the seine net. Later, I estimated our following at about 700 birds. When Kenn, for my obvious amusement, slung a gut high in the air, the strident din was terrific but the whole spectacle as an exhibition of concentrated flying was truly remarkable. Nor was Kenn satisfied until he had got four gulls doing an aerial tug-of-war over the one gut, with every other pair of wings wheeling to the attack.

Some greater black-backed gulls observed the proceedings warily from a little distance, while still farther out floated several gannets or solan geese apparently unconcerned with our fishing. When you come on a gannet asleep on the ocean, said the skipper, he lets out an unholy screech. A few fulmars passed swiftly—known locally as the "St. Kilda Maa".

But now the starboard rope was nearly out and I was throttling back; round she came and over went the net, with the glass balls bouncing away after knocking on the stern board crisp and neat as flying feet in a fantastic ballet; and now the net was out, and round once more I brought her, opening throttle as the port rope slid over, on the run back for the dan.

I am quite sure that the dawn that morning must have been more wonderful, more vivid and beautiful, than most dawns that I have seen, but—for I try to be truthful here—I have no clear memory of it. All I see is a molten red, a red that is dazzling me. I cannot pick up the dan. I am steering blind, but haven't the courage to confess it. I could have swept that sun with pleasure from the sky. But I hold on, for I know that I must be roughly on course. Then I glimpse in a vanishing moment what seems a slim dark finger upright in the heart of the red and, with a breath of relief, I keep her dead on the rising sun.

June Light

All in all, June, I think, is the most perfect month for the West Coast. Not only, as a rule, does it provide the best weather, but, above everything, it provides light. It is the month of light, of every kind of light, from the white of noonday, with the cattle knee-deep in water over the pale sands, to the elfin-green hillocks of midnight. The light sleeps under blue skies, races in silver over racing seas, or fades away into mist and gloom. If it holds to bright sunshine in windless weather for many days on end, one is struck by this marvel of constancy, and when folk meet they exclaim about it. It is like a living legend. Then shadow comes. The skies cloud over. The wind blows up. Here is the grey rain. What a pity that the weather has at last broken!

And then one goes out into this weather and experiences the

softness of the small rain, sees the mists trailing over the mountains, shelters under a bluff from the hurrying drenching shower, feels the fragrant wind that gives to the skin—even the oldest skin—a smoothness as of velvet, is touched by an eddy of scent, of bog myrtle, of honeysuckle, and, looking abroad upon the vast and ever-changing scene, recognizes, in a swift access of assurance, that this at last is the real West Coast.

What matter that to-morrow's trip to a neighbouring island may have to be cancelled? To-morrow will look after itself, every to-morrow will look after itself. . . .

And then—it's to-morrow and lo! instead of a further extension of bad weather, the sun occupies his swept heaven, and earth and sea rejoice as if they had been reborn.

The seashore is a continuous delight, with its rock-pools and translucent bathing bays and ribbed sands, where you dig up cockles. In June, too, its bird life is interesting, for the young are about and the parents properly protective. You can watch an eider-duck family for an hour . . . and wake up to the vacant water lazily moving around or breaking upon rocks and skerries.

One of these islands I hold to be the most beautiful of all the islands in the West. Its shape varies according to the angle of approach but can never be mistaken because of the rock, so well known to geologists, that crowns it. This long high ridge sometimes looks like the keel of an upended boat and sometimes like the dorsal fin of a gigantic sea monster. Buzzards nest there and ravens croak against its dark walls, while the uplands leading to it carry more wheatears and stonechats than I have ever seen elsewhere in any one place. But what distinguishes the island for me and holds it fragrant in memory is the wild Scotch rose (*Rosa spinosissima*), for it blooms here in greater abundance than anywhere else I know. It is the genius of this place. It grows near the seashore, on banks, in clefts, but above all on the little green braes bordered with hazel woods. It rarely reaches more than two feet in height; in colour, neither white nor cream so much as mellow old ivory; unassuming, modest, and known as the white rose of Scotland.

For me it has a fragrance more exquisite than that of any other rose. It drifts upon rather than strikes the senses, like the fragrance from a presence. It is soft and pervasive but dwells in its own place. Like the colour of the old-ivory petals it comes from a far time, with the matured perfection which we sometimes glimpse in a jade dragon ring carved three thousand years ago by a Chinese artist concerned, with infinite skill and prolonged discipline, to fashion his emblem of heaven. It has that aristocratic quietism of a perfected timeless art, and it has the freshness of a country girl's sun-bleached, new-laundered linen. Upon sense and being it confers the rare moment of harmony.

Never before had I found this part of the world so full of light, so peaceful, so beautiful. As we sailed away heavy clouds massed on the Cuillin, on the peaks of Inverness-shire, on Ben More in Mull; Ardnamurchan, Caliach Point, the Dutchman's Hat and Coll lay in a faint haze. But these Inner Isles were in a ring of light.

The Heart of the Deer Forest

She slips out and opens the iron gate in the deer fence. I drive through. She locks the gate and comes back to her seat. The world and all its doings have been padlocked off, and the gears slide home on a chuckle of acceleration.

The last inhabited house is already miles behind, and the deserted keeper's cottage where we are going to stay is three miles in front. No one is waiting to receive us.

There is a freedom, a loneliness, that is pure exhilaration. And our old friends, the mountain hares, are here already. They come charging off the moor on to the narrow road and then hit out hell-for-leather in front of us. Their ears have still the trick of throwing one forward and one back at the same time, particularly when I'm on their tails. For I must find out whether they have allowed themselves to degenerate in the matter of speed. No, they are still keeping old Nature's flag at the mast-head, for the full-grown lad immediately in front is doing his generous thirty miles an hour.

"That will do!" pleads a voice; but I shout encouragement

through the windscreen. And then, whisk! the noble fellow has come to his side alley and is off the road. We catch a glimpse of him slowing up as he lopes, head ridiculously aloft, to his little brown home on the moor. I try to explain the sort of thrill he gets out of this and how, at a certain mad season, he boasts about it.

At first I wondered just how one of these mountain hares sees this particular part of the world in his head, and fancied he sees it as we might the ground-plan of a modern city. Naturally enough a hare would no more think of barging through water-laden peat-hags than we through the walls of houses. So when he observes a monstrous noisy apparition coming charging across the moor, he may feel that his best way of getting to safety is not by rushing off vaguely into hinterlands of hags and swamps but by first reaching the main street of his ground-plan, racing along that until he comes to his own side street, and then whisking off broadway and so home to pant in his own native corner. Anyway, that's how a great number of them have gone home before us. Always excepting the fellow who, in the mist, missed his side street. That was a heroic business for though he was not fully grown he touched 27 m.p.h. by the speedometer. So fine an effort made me obediently stop the car for a few minutes to give him time to find his bearings.

But before top gear was engaged again, there he was plumb on the middle of the road and, at a first glimpse, amplified into the father of all hares for visibility now was barely a matter of twenty yards. When he saw us, off he lolloped in front once more. Nothing I could do by way of sudden acceleration, siren-hooting, or waiting with engine cut out would get that hare off the road. When at last we stopped before the cottage, he stopped. I walked slowly towards him. But at five yards, he hopped on, obviously very tired, but also as it were strangely astonished. After a little while he was nowhere to be seen. The more I thought about this problem in behaviour the more intricate it became, particularly in that strange region beyond the human analogy.

But that was on a previous visit. Here in the clear light the grouse rocket up, crying what sounds like "Go-back! Go-back!" but is in reality nothing so polite. The sarcasm in an old cock's voice can be pretty thick or hard as he rolls like a boat in a sea. I like that roll as he disappears over the crest. The real sailor of the moor, with business at every little port; but capable of going down the roaring forties like a dark thunderbolt.

The hawk, the eagle, the peewit, the curlew, the linnet, the solitary elusive cry in the half-dark of the golden plover. We'll see and hear them all.

And the hills! We know their shape; the uplift, the down-sweep, the flow of them; each by name, in that silence of intimacy that comes very near the dark speechless centres. The corries, like hollows in the mountains' throats; below the corries, the foothills; then the slow dark brown swell of the moor as it dips to the river.

The eye lifts to the highest mountain again, to Morven; a shapely simple mountain. Anyone can climb it with ease. But the other year it gave us a vision of the cauldron that smokes from a nether world. We had had the wild notion of watching the sun rise beyond the Orkneys and set off about ten o'clock at night. Round two in the morning we were somewhere on or near the peak, with what seemed a precipice just beyond our feet, and up that precipice the mist boiled in dark convolutions that were fearsome enough to give body to childhood visions of the Christian hell. We retreated very very carefully, and when we won back to the cottage her legs, she said, were attached by no more than two slender threads.

Now we catch a fair view of the small river. Some water in it, too. I see the spot where I tailed my first salmon. We were on the left bank and as the angler brought the tired fish round, I, lying flat on my stomach, had to lean over the shallow bank, catch the tail—or rather the slim part above it—in my left hand and heave the fish up and over my body. I was surprised at how easily this was done. We were also a little surprised that the salmon was certainly no more than eight pounds, but then we mightn't have been, for experience had taught us that a fish which has been up river for a while takes a long time to show himself and any angler may be excused for thinking he has got into something big.

The trout run about four to the pound, though the half-pounder has been caught. But reflections are snipped by a cry and there is the pale gable-end of the cottage itself, the solitary cottage lost in the heart of the deer forest. The eyes switch and, yes, on the green meadowland between cottage and river are the hinds, heads up in that lovely grace of astonishment. It is not that they move so much as that movement runs among them. I cannot readily think of any movement in nature that is at once more subtle and tentative, more enchanting. We can wind our silver horn of acknowledgement only by pressing the car's hooter. They scatter and are gone.

The gardener goes too, for she has a bank into which she stuck last year some plants gathered off the moor. We have arrived.

The Solitary Crofter

It may seem absurd—as it probably is—to say that an intelligent eye could, looking over a crofting community, tell the characters of the crofters from the condition of their crops. But here the hay is cut first, there last; here the fields are clean, there rather choked and dirty; here the crops are in a forward state, there they are late—with all gradations of time and tidiness and carelessness between the extremes. The farthest-away croft is always last in harvesting any crop, and there were times last year when we smiled at what seemed the sheer optimism of the man who works it. He was sowing his turnip seed—the early part of the season had been abnormally dry—so late that he could hardly expect to get results worth bothering about. Occasionally we could see him working all alone on an upland, slowly, in a timeless sort of way, as if the idea of haste had never touched the primeval order of his thought. Then one day, meeting him at the end of a row, near the path, I stopped and we fell into talk. His voice was low and quiet and gentle. Och, something would come of it. There would be turnips all right.

Maybe it was a little late, but then . . . He smiled. Whatever it was it would be no more than he would expect. And if it wasn't that—then perhaps it wouldn't be. "I have no one to help me." He did not sound helpless so much as rather remote and vaguely uncaring. But pleasant. He lived all alone. His eyes once or twice became friendly and alight as if he were privileged by the talk. He sounded simple in the way that land and crops are simple. Nothing at all dark or dour, as some make out the primeval to be. And I knew that however long I stood there, he would stand also.

At the moment his hay is gathered in small ricks over the field. His corn is still green (it is harvested elsewhere) but in due course it will come to maturity and whiten. Then it will be cut. In stook it will stand for many days, accept blatters of rain, and, bedraggled, half-collapse. But the dry wind will blow up, and the sun shine after frosty mornings, and in the fullness of time the old horse that stands by the corner of the little barn, with drooping head and the main weight on one hind leg, will be hitched to the sledge and the harvest brought slowly home.

Probably he is a bit of a by-word with his neighbours—but not in any unfriendly way. Some wag among them, with the customary dry humour, will have characterized him as "not exactly pushing". That will raise a smile—with a slight touch of wonder for that which remains outside time and crisis and any undue concern with personal gain. The practical, hard-working, earnest mind will finally dismiss him, however, as a somewhat futile antique in a busy real world.

But there is a kind of mind in which a certain sympathy, a friendly interest, is roused. Granting that such sympathy may be over-facile, yet I am not sure but that it springs from a deep primordial mood, however difficult it may be to search out with any certainty.

In one's writing of the world of Nature there is always, of course, the danger of the facile thought, of the "poetic" phrase. It is as well, perhaps, to experience a mood or emotion more than once before risking its expression. Beyond the west boundary of this man's croft the land folds over in little green braes, clad with juniper and brier and other low bushes. It is a haunt of rabbits and small singing birds. The turf is always close-cropped, and in the little alleyways between the bushes one may lie on a sunny day and have the oddest thoughts. And not always mere thought; a vague expectancy rather than thought, and touched now and then with the least suggestion of the panic—in the antique sense; a pleasant complex mood of detachment, of intimacy. I would not wish to overload the fantasy by introducing a goat, but in fact there is frequently a goat there or thereabouts, and we look at each other from a little distance. I know him well.

A burn wanders down by these little braes and has on its right bank a solitary birch-tree. The trunk leans out over the water, before going straight up. Not a large tree, but we see the spring there, the fullness of summer, then the pale gold that glows as with sunlight on the dullest day, and finally the delicate bare twigs that turn black in the gloaming against a wintry sky.

There is also a solitary Scots fir and if you stand beside it when the wind blows you hear the sea. There are many other ordinary simple things on or by the croft of the man who may be observed at odd times working on his upland fields all alone and as if time were long and calm as eternity.

The Rose at the Gable-end

A dark-red rose grows at the gable-end of the house, by the inner corner. We are not quite sure of its name, for in the years it has grown to a tall bush, with the blooms on a level with the face, as if it aspired to be a climber. Its scent is rich but not cloying, for just when it is going to be too rich a penetrating tang right from the core of the red darkness induces a small shiver—and recoil.

The mind cannot get used to this scent, to the sheer wonder of it. In sunlight and in darkness, first the scent and then the keener, darker tang that comes from the core of the rose, the concentration of fragrance, its life's essence that may not quite be borne.

Sometimes I am astonished at the amount of pleasure or delight which in a forgetful mood one passes by on the other side. For days on end one forgets all about the bush, and then, in some odd moment, fingers lift a new bloom that has reached its hour of perfection, and lo!

But one does learn to grow cunning about it. When the brain is weary or the job difficult, when "world tragedy" becomes more than a locution, one can always leave the room or come in at the gate, go round the garden and see how the vegetables are growing, the fruit ripening, and, by way of afterthought, pause to look at the rose-bush, to look at one particular rose, to keep on looking at it.

For a certain amount of deliberation is necessary. One can cultivate surprise, just as one can cultivate onions. Let there be nothing mysterious about this. Every sense can be trained. Appreciation can be deepened. The first magical surprise at sight of a lovely thing need not be the last nor the profoundest. There may be an element in the first surprise that cannot be recaptured but even that I doubt. Indeed I would be untrue to the rose at the gable-end if I did not say frankly that to me never has it blown with such surprise and beauty as it has this year.

But then I have discovered an extra method of approach to it.

The habit of taking a walk round part of the house and out perhaps as far as the gate before going to bed some time around midnight, can become deep-rooted. Often it is so dark that I find myself groping for the door on coming in lest I stub my nose. Even when the weather is all worked up to a slashing rain-storm, at least the door must be opened for a last look. Many would feel uncomfortable if they went to bed without washing their teeth.

So the habit is not irksome. Habit rarely is. One can look forward to it as only the lucky these days can look forward, say, to a night-cap, to their favoured drink. Though "look forward" is hardly the proper expression; it comes normally in the fullness of the hour. And at least it has this advantage over the more delectable drinks, namely, that it is insusceptible of governmental regulation even of the most meaningless kind.

Realizing this, the weather on the whole does its best. While the roses bloom, whatever the wind may have been up to during the day, it tends to fall away at midnight to a complete silence. There is a hush on the face of the earth and the trees are dark against the sky. For a long period about the height of the year, a livid pallor, a weird afterglow, lingers in the heavens, and the dark tree-tops are a fantastic architecture, utterly still, against the light. You hold your breath and listen, and the trees listen with you, until you hear the silence.

If you listen to that silence for a long time, the body, quite on its own, may react in a small shiver, not the same shiver as comes from the scent of the rose, but part of the same realm of wonder.

An owl hoots in the trees by the edge of the park. The cry is blown out like a match in the darkness, and the silence deepens. There is a sudden heavy breath from an invisible cow lying down somewhere beyond the hedge. The owl calls again. Another answers. Far away there is a faint high crying of gulls, like a memory of distant seas. That startled crying passes.

As you listen, the body lightens, pervaded by the cool night air. All the congestions of the day drain away from the brain, yet you cannot get near enough to this night world, cannot quite become one with it, and in a lingering moment you wish you could, you wish you could apprehend that which just eludes you. If only you could manage to become one with it, something profound might be revealed.

Perhaps you do not really think this; rather you feel the thought of it, and in this involuntary feeling there is a certain measure of communion, so that even though you remain ignorant of any final apprehension, there is yet something inside you that raises a faint smile of humour or irony, not at all sad or sombre, but instinct with our strange mortality, our undismayed acceptance of our lot.

For real thought, any intellectual effort, at such a moment is all wrong. Let the body become receptive as an instrument. Let the night, the hidden sounds, the trees and the sky, play on it. Why should we always be pestering it with inquiry and regulation, philosophy and science? Throw all this truck of pride and the daily round away, like a game played too long, far too long and too earnestly. Give the body we treat so indifferently its one full minute. And the mind will join with the body in this cool night bath, and they will turn away refreshed and better friends.

Turn away and cross the corner of the lawn to the rose-bush, in conspiracy now, both of them. The rose is dark, but the eye imagines it sees the deep red flame in the darkness. The petals are cool to the fingers. And the scent, more hidden than in the sunlight, is here, still here, and then, in a swift divine instant, the concentration of fragrance from the red core.

At this point I thought I would test a recent gift I got, consisting in two volumes of a *Dictionary of Quotations and Proverbs*, and under "Rose" I find no fewer than eighteen entries. Now for the distilled wisdom and beauty of all the ages! But as I look up reference after reference I remain dissatisfied. A rose by any other name would no doubt smell as sweet, and it's sad about the last rose of summer left blooming alone. Shakespeare is clever and Moore nostalgic. Wordsworth's "budding rose above the rose full blown" is a perfect picture. Yeats's "Far off, most secret, and inviolate Rose" is profound and mystical, but not quite the rose at the gable-end, not the rose that human fingers take the liberty to touch and draw near. Scott's rose is "fairest when 'tis budding new" and "sweetest washed with morning dew". "As though a rose should shut and be a bud again" is Keats doing his natural magic. Milton has his "flowers of all hue, and without thorn the rose".

In vain I hunt among the quotations for the words that had come into my own mind:

"Oh, my luve's like a red, red rose."

Perhaps not many of us have been lucky enough to have had a love like that. Or is it that we are not capable of seeing our love like that when we have her?

But it's no use! Something extra seems missing from the

quotations somewhere, some red-rose background out of which the rose itself comes, some immanence of rose as actual as its scent—and as pervasive and continuing. Even the simple memory of a wood fire can fill the whole mind.

So let us get back to the blessedly tangible, for there was a spell during July when dashing rains so tattered the buds that they had all they could do to struggle into more than half-being. Yet even for these—there is no getting to the bottom of this matter—the gardener herself had a special glance. They certainly were poor things. "What a shame!" And if the words sounded like an oblique reflection upon the First Cause, well, why wouldn't they? There are times when it is as well to take a firm stand with the rose against all comers, immanent or otherwise.

And in the fullness of time the rose dies. We utter the words as softly and glibly as if that were the end of the matter. But it's not the end of the matter for the gardener. A watchful eye will be kept on the bush through the winter. Its roots will be warmed by an application of that which they like to feed upon. And the rose will come again as sure as summer's self.

I must even confess that I write this about the rose while I sit on a chair before the evening fire. You who may read these words do not see the rose as you read. Where is this rose that neither of us sees—yet can almost put a hand on?

Sometimes I do declare I am more moved by the rose in memory than by the actual rose on the bush. Sometimes. But the rose has to be on the bush before it can be in the memory. There's the perfect rub. And for those who want a moral there's the moral too, for when you think of things we are supposed to get morals from, would you exclude the rose?

And the moral in this case is so simple. Nothing more than: Look at the rose. But—*look* at it. Bend towards it. Salute it. Then, at another time, look at it again.

Hill Shadows

From the door of the fishing hut, the ground sloped gently for about a hundred yards to the brow of the hill, which went sheer down some 1,300 feet into the glen—and rose again as steeply on the opposite side to about the same height, whereupon it fell back in long upward slopes to the crest of Beinn Dearg (3,547 feet). Beinn Dearg is saddle-backed, with a bluff face to the left, and from the hut appears to be in the centre of a line of somewhat similar smooth-humped mountains, so that one might have found it hard to say which of six or seven crests was the highest, did not Beinn Dearg so often betray itself by a solitary cloud-cap. In the intense bright sunlight of midsummer noons, these hills are not impressive in size; indeed, to the eye by the hut, they are smooth and exposed as the backs of great, crouching, innocent animals that a giant hand might at any moment caress. They are green in the sun, green with an olive grey, and solitary clouds that sail in the sky cast dark moving shadows upon them.

It is a delight to watch these shadows that sometimes move like ships with drowsy slowness, but often in shape are not like ships, but have a nucleus and irregular arms like twisted starfish, or filmy outblown thoughts of starfish. These shadows descend into the corries, pass over smooth breasts, lie upon the flanks of

Gleann na Sguaib, climb and undulate, touch the base of Beinn Dearg, move over the great couchant body, until the last arm is lingeringly withdrawn and the bluff face is left full on its sleepy chin. Gleann na Sguaib is rather a narrow glen whose stream rises under that sleepy chin and comes at right angles to the main glen until it is lost in the head waters of Loch Broom. The stream and a light-brown road run companionably together, but the tribe of McNabs that once used them were evicted in a body long ago and now no human dwelling distracts the eye.

During the day sunshine and shadow keep up their endless play on these mountains; but with evening the colour changes to a strange darkened eerie green; deepening to dark velvet, until the western side becomes like a living hide ever approaching and spreading. The tops are now in mist; purple and withdrawn, the mountains become great in size, are changed from sleepy animals to primordial gods. Their shrouded heads have a still menace, though they are too vast, too withdrawn, to know menace consciously. Something heedless and uncanny about them, yet austere and fixed as doom. When a man gets this vision he is struck by the immobility he beholds, and breaks it with a physical shudder, and turns away, strengthened and humbled no doubt, but also with some queer secret elation in him that hunts instinctively for a rhythm. On their own, his nostrils start humming over a closed mouth—a mouth that opens now and then to take the breaking surge of the rhythm on cold lips—a fragment of melody older than the Gaels perhaps, older than the little dark pre-Gael men possibly, old as these mountains that have withdrawn themselves from the play of sun and wind to the integrity of their primordial natures.

Every evening the glen changes, and one of its most interesting expressions is provided by the night clouds when, below the level of the hut where the air is clear, they form the even surface of a vast sea-inlet. Immediately below, perhaps, the surface is discernible as cloud, but on the right towards Braemore, and on the left towards Ullapool, it is grey-white as night-water, flowing into mountain ravines and uprising there in sea-spouts. But when the rain comes and the mountains are seen only for moments in the lightening and darkening of heavy clouds, then the glen provides the infernal picture of a vast chasm whose rock faces gleam dully red in light diffused from a sinking sun.

For it is not always sun and shadow on these hills. Indeed the most remarkable thing about this world of vast immobile bulk is its love of change. When at noon the wind dies and the sun vanishes and the rain comes noiselessly down, the stillness grows awful and impersonal. The silence is the silence before life itself; and out of it lifts a primeval mountain-head that glooms and fades. The small burn by the door of the hut invades this silence with the sound of a perpetual falling into a cauldron. It is a world of fantastic deception, of unreal terrors. Coming down on the hut with a bag of peat, one is suddenly confronted by the brow of the hill across the glen rising to a terrifying height into the cloud—yet that brow, regarded so often, cannot be on a very much higher level than the hut. This illusion for a moment takes the breath. It can hardly be the brow with its familiar scree below, it must be mighty Beinn Dearg itself; yet no, it is the brow beyond doubt, rising to that dark, dizzying height like a rampart against heaven.

During the day now the valley below is invaded by cloud, solid white cloud assuming all shapes. A great white dragon has that brow in its open jaws; an island of cloud throws a white fountain-spout from its midst; curtains come down shutting out all.

We set out for the uncharted loch on the slopes of Meall a' Chairn in a stillness emphasized by the burn as though it were the invisible other-world machinery producing it. As we leave this noisy burn behind, the stillness becomes the deathly negation of all life. There are not even the midges which such damp windlessness so readily and evilly produces. It is a stillness in which it is no use fishing or otherwise pursuing any aim. Yet we go on, as though we had to go, driven out from our shelter to seek the lost essence of life in this lifeless waste. The peaty ground is boggy and tufted with heather and hill grass and wild flowers. For a moment the jagged peaks of An Teallach, like splintered teeth, show dimly through cloud-wrack beyond Dundonnell, then fade out. Far to the left, amid hill-tops, a small loch shows wan and incredible. A curtain of mist is approaching it, the thick foot of the curtain bunching visibly under the drag of the heathery ground. The loch so slowly vanishes that one can see it in the mist when it is gone. Looking back a moment after we do see it like a reflection—or do we? In another moment all the hills there have gone and the curtain is advancing over the near breast above the Fairy Loch with its green reeds. Spots of real rain begin to fall. We seek shelter against a rock on the edge of one of these innumerable low ridges that give mountainous ground its character. The rain comes down in thin white lances, straight down, like rays from a ghostly sun. Still no midges. No life. Shall we go on or back? Decision is sucked by the dumb boggy ground. The rain is soft and not at all cold; it has *feel* rather than wetness. The spread-out coat gathers little pools; a neglected shoulder gets wet through without making any effort to cover itself. Rain continues for an hour. Why, in any case, should it ever stop? Whether we go on or back—what does it matter? This lifeless-ness is not unpleasant. For a moment indeed some secret point of pleasure gleams far in the mind at this withdrawnness—where nothing can reach from the world behind. The advancing curtain loses its close texture as it passes over us so that our near vision is little affected.

Then all at once in this soft rain-silence there is the chirping of small birds. We see them down below us. They are excited as if they were fearful for their young. Their chirp is like the sparrow's, but firmer and clearer. There is a soft flap of wind in

153

the rock at our backs and a large bird flies out noiselessly. The small birds mob it. Clearly from the wing-shape it is not a hawk. Possibly an owl. It flies steadily away out of sight. The rain is now falling not so heavily, its lances all but invisible in the grey light. We may as well go on. The uprising ground is soft but tufted more firmly with strong hill-grass, amid which the heather is pale-budded and the cross-leaved heath in full bloom. There are many shades of this heath from a wan pink through scarlet to purple. We are lucky enough to stumble on white. The bog asphodel, yellow and bronze, is everywhere full-blown. Yellow tormentil, purple loosestrife, stonecrop and woodruff, lilac thyme, orchis pale pink to purple, the curled leaves greeny-yellow of the butterwort not yet in flower, the white canna (sometimes with one flag, more often with four), a saxifrage with clusters of yellowish-green flowers on a rocky watercourse, and everywhere the ever-varying richness of close-packed moss from green to dark red, a carpet of unobtrusive yet magnificent colouring.

We slowly climbed the slopes of the Meall searching for the uncharted loch, where monstrous fish are said to abide. We found it—and at the first glance thought it the most beautiful of all the lochs. Though beautiful is a word that can hardly be used here—in any circumstances. Some vague breath of wind has darkened all its surface except for the wide glassy margin round its sides; but when we stand by its edge the darkening hardly appears to be the effect of immediate wind as of a wind that died long ago. The rain grows heavy again and pelts the surface. This loch seems uncanny and unmapped, yet in some way, more than any of the others, it has memories of the world. Perhaps this is because, instead of the usual all-round mossy margin, it has along its southern shore low rocky headlands. Through the mist these give the illusion of a rockbound sea-coast in miniature. Yet that very illusion of worldly association withdraws it all the more from the real world as by a magical trick. No sense in fishing here; less sense in gazing. We turn back.

And then down among some hags in this grey weather tragedy sets its middle scene. An unshorn ewe has fallen into a round hole half-full of water from which she struggles to escape. Her lamb in desperate fear watches the struggle from the bank. The bog sucks the ewe deeper after each spasmodic effort to climb the black soapy wall. Then suddenly the lamb sees death and in a mad terror takes to the hillside, bleating wildly. There is something so extraordinarily like the behaviour of a child in the lamb's actions, the child fleeing in elemental fear from what it loves most, that for a moment the world animate and inanimate beats with one pulse.

The ewe with her heavy fleece is so deeply bogged that our efforts to lift her are completely futile. She no longer struggles. Her head settles down with a dreadful expressionless quiescence. We tear away the soft wall of peat with our hands, scoop and trench, until by slow degrees we drag the sodden body on to firm ground. Her hind legs now lie stretched behind her as if they were broken. There are flies and a stench. The lamb is against the skyline, bleating wildly as ever, but looking back, running and looking back. We are sodden with sweat and bog water, and bitten by gnats. The ewe won't get to her feet, however we struggle with her. Time passes. Then all at once, as if the will and the strength had come at the same moment from some mysterious place, she is on her feet and walking away with scarcely a stumble. The lamb sees her and circles madly round the near horizon. And an odd relief, like a kindly ironic smile, comes down over the face of that soft grey world.

Mo Dhachaidh

We have been on the move again and seen the mountain ranges of Ross and Inverness from the western sea; have listened to the tapping of an oyster-catcher's chick inside the shell; have watched an eider-duck family from the cliff-top of a Hebridean island as they dived and played round a low sea rock while our hostess told us how she once observed three young otters sport in that same spot. It was the first time she had ever seen otters in their native environment, and obviously the scene had made a lively impression.

How vast, and how minute, the objects of interest for the eye! Oigh-sgeir lighthouse is about the size of a human finger on the remote horizon, seen one moment and gone the next. The spinning-jenny at one's feet is stuck to a piece of old heather so that it is all but indistinguishable from it. The great rock pinnacle high above the breast of the moor is smoking like some gargantuan factory chimney as the clouds divide upon it and sweep round it, the dark of the rock seeming itself to move

156

like an inner black smoke. The wide floor of the sea, green over the sand, purple-brown over the tangle, and deepening blue into the far distance. And, beyond all, the horizons of the ocean and of the mountain ranges.

For the most part the weather was wet, but often when the rain ceased and the clouds hung low there would come into the air a soft, divine warmth, full of fragrance. The sun would pierce through, and all the world would fill with light; brim and tremble and spill over, and off sped the light over the grass and in among the wild roses and glittering across the sea. The sheer freshness of such a moment had surely the spirit of creation in it, a first creation.

It is not merely that the world there is quiet and full of peace to the war-worn mind. It is far more than that, for in the stillness if you listen you can hear life breathe and grow. The moment is positive. You feel that this world here is not only immensely old, but that it is living now—otter and eider-duck, grass and wild rose—with a deep inexhaustible fullness of life, and will go on living, in sun and rain and storm and fragrance, into immense time. You feel in it a profound naturalness.

Even to lie on the cliff-top watching the sea as it plays round the otters' rock, in slow impulses from a brimming fullness, idly, carelessly, but unceasingly, is to wonder if creation itself had not something of the game at the core of its first impulse.

You pass through a rift of honeysuckle. You stand for a moment on a tumbling green brae and wonder what this scent is now, and then your eyes pick up the low-growing bushes of the wild Scotch rose. The ivory petals are wet; your hands get wet; your feet are wet, and your face; so you bother no more with wetness, but stand and move idly, time and weather being no great matter, or the essence of everything—as you like.

Cattle move across the foreshore. The hay is waiting to be cut. Little fields are green with young corn. The ferry-boat that meets the steamer is lying at anchor in the flow of the tide.

Sea-birds cry and swoop at you as you head for the low skerries and the white sands. They make far more of a row than is necessary; are obviously overdoing their maternal or paternal concern, working up their emotions to a grand old pitch. It's not often they get the chance! But after you've been lying down for a time the old oyster-catcher sits on a rock at a little distance, lowers his head into his neck, watches you with one eye and goes to sleep with the other.

Sailing past great cliff walls, in which slim waterfalls are like veins of quartz. Cormorants on a skerry off the headland, sunning their wings and looking like miniature black eagles. And then, as we enter the sound, a sudden wash of breaking seas a short distance to port. What can be the cause of that? Our boatman, who knows these seas better than the city man his streets, says, "Basking sharks." After a little while a triangular fin does cut the surface, but the sport is under the water. Presently a small one, perhaps twelve feet or so in length, breaks surface quite close to us, but immediately dives and makes off.

But what are those white specks on the mountainside of the approaching island? They weren't there last year. The boatman smiles a peculiar and knowing smile. "Sheep," he says.

"Sheep? On this forbidden island!"

He nods.

So we nod, too, and smile. Things in this world have occasionally a habit of coming full circle, if you wait long enough!

There was the old story of the hundreds of crofters who had been cleared off this island, which in due course was turned into a deer forest—indeed into a sort of sporting paradise, complete with brand-new castle and all. The castle is still there, and the estate workers' houses, but the grass is growing long on the lawns, and silence hangs about the winding avenues. The sacred land has been let to a distant sheep farmer, who has introduced over 2,000 sheep to the mountain slopes.

This is indeed something to reflect upon, as the shearwaters rise on fast-beating wings, dip and bank, touching the sea surface with the tip of a wing. And there, all in a moment, no less than seven gannets; and here, at hand, a solitary puffin scuttering away with an air of foolish surprise that raises a smile.

Is there anything more pleasant in the world of travel than sailing by islands in distant seas, gazing at sandy bays on wild uninhabited coasts, pumping the primus for a cup of tea, enjoying friendly company, taking a turn at the tiller, always moving, always with the eyes roving and steadying, seeing that which is at once familiar and strange?

And so at last we come to our farthest island, which lies to the sun, and has potatoes and strawberries long before we have them on the mainland. And cream, too. And the cream of hospitality forbye. It is an attractive place to reach, with its sheltered bay and its cultivated land, and the bright, airy house with the sloping garden.

So many things have to be inspected and discussed. The new boat in particular. The hours slip away, and here, in no time, we are waving to host and hostess as they climb the beach and pass the small coal dump and the little church.

So it's home now to our own island, to the long green evening, with logs burning brightly in the flat open fireplace, and good cheer and good spirit going around.

The day we left was one of those perfect days that, falling upon the Hebrides at any odd time, are for ever memorable. Travelling then by sea in a halcyon calm, one stands on the steamer's top deck and becomes imbued by the fabulous nature of this western world. The islands take upon them the stillness of a dream. Colour softens and holds the eyes like a memory one does not care to define, like a memory one could never define, so that it has a wash of emotion faint as the farthest purple that fades into the haze.

A whale crosses our wake, shouldering the sea slowly. Gulls

balance overhead, white as sleep. All at once there is the cry of the pipes from somewhere for'ard.

The captain tells me that the piper is a Canadian who many years ago emigrated with his mother and six brothers and sisters from one of the Outer Isles. He was a young lad then, but the family set to and cleared the virgin land, and they were now doing quite well. His brother was on board also. They were both in Air Force blue.

His fingering is not too sure. Phrases are slurred a little. But after a time he settles down to a tune and plays it with a fine deliberation. I know every note of it, but cannot for the moment recall its name.

Presently I fall into talk with him and he tells me that he has not played for a long time, though as a lad in the Islands he had learned properly. I ask him the name of the tune.

"'Mo dhachaidh'," he says. "'My home'." And adds: "It was looking at those hills."

Travelling has its difficulties and snags in these days. The mainland can bring us back with a bump to what we call "reality". By the time we reached Fort William in the afternoon we were pretty hungry, not having eaten since the early morning. Getting a seat on a bus is not always easy, but with half an hour on hand we should manage something and are recommended to a fashionable café. We enter the eating-room and wait. No one pays us any attention. Time passes. I turn to look towards a ginger-haired waitress who seems to be counting spoons. Perhaps she did not notice us come in? Presently she leaves her task and, coming directly to us, informs us that she has much more to do than attend to us. Her voice and manner are rude and waspish. In her excess of ill-temper she tugs at the window curtain and goes back to her task of counting spoons. We had never opened our mouths. We get up and leave that place, and as I pass the cash desk down below I have to explain that, having been given nothing to eat, we have nothing to pay.

MO DHACHAIDH

It was a far cry from the friendliness of the islands and the steamer's deck. We let that pass, with the hope that the stranger in the future would have better luck, particularly if he had heard of what is called "Highland hospitality".

But we had a grand trip behind us, with work done, and renewed hope in the future of that land which to so many wandering on the surface of the world will always be "Mo dhachaidh".

The Gentle Rain from Heaven

I fancy I can hear the ground drinking in the rain, drinking it in with a myriad dry upturned mouths like the mouths of lambs. The morning is completely windless, and through the mist in the glen I can dimly see the outline of the ridge on the other side, with here and there a vaguely shrouded solitary tree. All is still and thundery warm, and the rain is coming straight down, not pelting but steady and even, in a monotony that is like a consummated ecstasy. The long leaves of the cherry-tree hang like hard feathers, and now one, now another, moves on its stem as it is hit by a raindrop. So a hen settles down to abide the rain, its head sunk, with now and then a faint meditative croak and a blinking of its round bright eye.

I can feel the rain doing good, can see the thin pale delicate roots of the ear of grain, of the grass, of the potato and lettuce and strawberry, of everything that grows absorbing this drink from heaven, after the long drought that has baked the clay to rock, with a slow swelling enrichment. The waiting fruits will stir now within themselves, will get busy, prepare for enlargement.

The grieve will be pleased. I met him last night when I went out to have a turn round after the midnight news. He was keeping his eye on a couple of mares about to foal. The fields were looking richly green in the evening light, but "Oh, we could be doing with a drop of rain!" I told him of a farm I had visited some days before in the West. One whole hayfield had been literally burnt brown. There would be no crop on it. We looked at the sky. Indications of rain had been there for two or three days but none had come, as if the sky through long abstinence had lost the natural art of raining. As I turned away a thrush started singing, or perhaps a blackbird, for the notes were rich and mellow rather than urgent. It was exactly half an hour after midnight, new time. I tapped the glass. It was still steady. But the bird may have had some premonition more subtle than the atmospheric influence which affects a weather glass.

From my trip to the West, I had brought back some books of modern poetry from a man who finds in poetry a natural enrichment of life. Sometimes I must confess I read this "modern" poetry with the same sort of reluctance with which I approach a crossword puzzle. Once I get going it's not so bad. There is some intellectual excitement, and one spots the economic leftish influences, the travail of the mind in subtle European embroilments of ideologies and what not, the clever learned allusions, the personal fun that remains obscure because you do not know the poet's friends or clique, the momentary but thick self-complacencies, and that ever-present air of disillusion, dry and arid but offhand. It never has a very enlivening effect, unless you happen to be interested in "new technique" for its own sake. And even if you are, new technique will not carry you all the way. Under the brazen sky, however splendid or terrifying to look upon, the delicate white roots, the hidden roots in the dark soil, slowly wither and die.

But among those I had brought back was one slender volume of poems by the Austrian, Rainer Maria Rilke, translated from the German by J. B. Leishman. This, I thought, will out-modern the modern young London men, for Rilke is admitted to be a prime influence upon most of them. This would be a very Torquemada among crossword puzzles. So I made an effort to get my mind to step out of its laziness, to gear up the intel-lectual apparatus, to prepare it for a maximum if short (for this can be tiring work) penetrative effort, to leap the untranslatable foreign words (after the manner of Ezra Pound) as nimbly as might be and still not leave go of some slender thread that I fancied I had got a hold of—in a word, to prepare myself for a battle which I was bound to lose.

And then Rilke's poetry fell like rain from heaven upon the arid place beneath. No intellectual strain searching for intel-lectual values, no vast effort in the head. A close absorbed atten-tion, an utter receptiveness, and down the rain falls, gently over the body and seeping deep into the blood. This is poetry and the magic of poetry, and it has been known of all time, for it is neither modern nor ancient but timeless. Time may give it its form and the spirit of the age its turn of phrase, perhaps, but the communication itself is timeless, and coming out of a last refinement of all experience it is not arrogant but gentle, gentle as the rain that falls on the dry ground.

When faith is restored in poetry, it is restored in humanity. Though "humanity" is little more than a lumpish word in the head, when it is not an ideal for which groups of men are pre-pared to commit the most fiendish atrocities. We all believe in humanity, especially the modern young poets. But this human-ity is so often humanity in the head. Not you or me, and the people we know, and the myriad individuals we don't know but who in all profound respects are like ourselves. The true poet's communication is individual, to one at a time. And one by one we become conscious of the gathering of ourselves in common understanding, in brotherhood. We know what it is to have understanding and sympathy. We go beyond ourselves, to a mouse, to a daisy. The most ordinary of us suddenly has his vision of the pale roots drinking in the rain, and he rejoices, and the work of the land is touched with wonder and mystery and happiness.

Not that I meant to mention these poets at all, for I have seen our North and West at their summer best. I have been to some remote parts of the West Coast, too, where this "time" business has become very confused. There are, in simple fact, three times, and we found all of them in use among different townships on Loch Torridon. When the appointed hour for the arrival of our ferry-boat had passed, we began wondering whether we had made it clear that it was the hour of the "new time" we had meant. The "new time" or steamer's time is two hours in advance of the Creator's time; the "old time" is one hour in advance; and of course there is basically and eternally the "Creator's time". In our simple way, we at last made up our minds that a mistake had been made, and that, with luck, we would have to wait only for the "old time". We were wrong, for there is a fourth time, the time that is outside all time and is "just a little late".

I have to report that the West is still yonder, with the green sea-water over its white sandy bays, as it has always been. On the rocks and skerries below the cliffs, the tide as usual had left pools of every shape and size and of every colour. From a plunge in a pool, the naked body squatted on a ledge and dried in a soft wind. A timid merganser drake and his less timid consort. Two gulls that swooped like dive-bombers to within a couple of feet of our heads. The three dark-mottled eggs of an oyster-catcher. Tufts of seapink in blossom. Caves, with a rich glory of marsh-marigolds upon the damp that oozes and drips.

I am trying to assure those whom it may concern that the lovelier parts of our Protected Area have not changed. They abide all our transitory issues. They knew human tragedies in the past, intense bitter holocausts local to themselves. Before I left I had a letter from a distinguished writer who has helped to free the tragic spirit in poetic drama. The war bears hardly on him (writes Gordon Bottomley) in preventing his getting to the North and West, and the Isles. "I am Antaeus to Scotland, and if it were to go on long I should fall into a real fright that my feet's lack of contact with that fertilizing earth would dry me up."

Antaeus, it will be remembered, the giant son of Gaea, the Earth, lost his power when his feet were parted from his mother, but whenever contact was renewed his strength returned.

We can't tell the Greeks much.

According to the gardener, however, one of the most delightful parts of a holiday, even a short one, is the coming back. Not but that it is full of concern and anxiety. Click goes the gate and out comes an exclamation at the serried ranks of daisies on the lawn. The mower will never do it! And the rockery—what a riot! And, oh lord, the goat has been in again. The two new wall roses—even the buds are eaten off, the brute! I am informed that it is too bad. Look at this! Look at that! But I go and look at my onions. I never grew them before. The leeks are tall and lanky. There is a flower on the new potatoes. A cry— the old cat has vanished and her kitten. I refrain from suggesting that the goat cannot be blamed for that. But I would require many pages to deal with the hungry beasts that gather around and my necessarily wary attitude towards them. Some sort of balance in nature has to be kept. I'm the dread keeper.

By midnight, I have attended to a few things and in a last look around am led to an outhouse where the old cat is purring over her offspring once more. We can close the door of our home now until the morning.

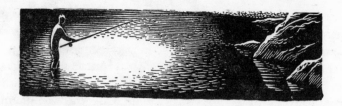

The Wilds of Sutherland

I have been doing little sums in arithmetic with petrol coupons and a road map. If the holiday could be arranged to start towards the end of one month and finish in the next, there might be a mild debauch of coupons, even though that would mean starvation before and after. It is an exciting thought that leads to an even more exciting question: Where, in the given circumstances, would one really like to go?

I submit that is a difficult question, not because it raises the very obvious matter of choice, but because it is essentially a secretive one. It has not so much the popular idea of holiday and enjoyment in it as some subtle need of physical and spiritual renewal. And if this seems a bit high-falutin, yet I remain convinced that at the core of every normal man or woman there lingers these days a desire for peace and renewal, however fugitively and whether actually indulged or not.

The real answer, I suppose, is the beautifully irrational one: Let us have a few days around so-and-so before we finally decide. So we headed for Lairg.

In a book that has just come into my possession, dealing with Caithness and Sutherland in the time of the Vikings, it is suggested that the country west and north of Lairg is pretty much what it was in the days of the Picts, and that it was very little inhabited even then, for the simple reason that a hundred acres of it would hardly support a sheep. This is very likely true. For there is about it a primeval atmosphere. But it is not a forbidding atmosphere—not, at least, to me. It does not overpower, as great inhuman mountain ranges do. There are no canyons, no sombre river gorges, nothing contorted into fantastic menace by some old earth god in a nightmare. There are mountains, but you first see them across spacious moors in one of a thousand different kinds of light. There may be an absence of humanity within that view, but that again may be no disadvantage, for humanity, like the poor (and we are mostly poor), we have always with us. So let cultural boastings and political ideologies get out of the view of the mountains. There will be mist enough presently, perhaps, an honest grey mist, and whether you curse it or endure it like a happy wanderer, there will be no two doubts about it—bless it!

The outstanding feature of this primeval land is that you can encompass it. You can take it to yourself and feel its strange wild intimacy. Or, if you like, you can let it take you. This, of course, is what is called "escape". The way we have changed the old heathen tabus, potent with feeling and imagery, into the modern "labels" which we call scientific, is a reasonable subject for mirth while the tea boils by a Sutherland loch. For, after all, from what does one escape—and into what? Mostly from an overdose of mass feeling or sensationalism into the forgotten reality of oneself. This reality may be a difficult thing to stand up to. But that's a different question—and I can guarantee that this region will provide the answer beyond any equivocal peradventure.

So to the road—"a comparatively good and a comparatively dull road", as one guide-book puts it—that runs its course across Sutherland from Lairg to the Laxford Bridge. Loch Shin is a long gut in that waste. I remember a youthful day when I push-biked it along with an Edinburgh lad who thought it, in a smirr of cold rain, so dreary a desolation that he judged it in that respect at least ultimate and final. Having imagination, he could pay tribute. It has midges and mosquitoes; it has horse-flies or clegs of a surpassing virulence—all in their season. It has trout, and some good trout. Guide-books say it is treeless, but that happens to be an exaggeration, for it has woods in parts. But it is not pretty, nor picturesque, nor sweet, nor charming, nor adorable. And if you are on foot, it seems without end. One of my happy memories is boiling a kettle by one of the little bushed and bouldered burns that run into it, on an evening of austere serenity; its timeless calm is likely to remain when many things that we fondly deem more ponderable, like a bank balance, will have gone.

But there was no need to linger so long by this loch, for there are the hill lochs that are hidden away from any main road. Guide-books never mention them. But they are there. Scores upon scores of them, lost in hinterlands where one can wander day after day without meeting a solitary soul. That does not mean that there are no gamekeepers. Many of these lochs, particularly in the west, have their fishing rights attached to hotels, and, well, they are not important enough, so to speak, to be expensively guarded. Hotel lochs are fished during the day, of course—when times are propitious. But there are countless lochs besides. And in any case, they look their loveliest or weirdest in the long summer evenings, or even longer summer mornings, when comfortable fishers are not yet astir.

But how to get there? Do so many miles up to a certain spot, leave the car, and come back with the midnight glimmer to sleep. Sleep where? Well, we sleep in our car, for it is a small car, but friendly, and flattens out its springy seats into two beds.

In any case, there is always a hotel or a simple "night accommodation" house. I know one such house, where the sea-birds, as I write, are calling along the sea inlet (later on the sea-trout will be running there) and, inland, the hill-birds are busy. Great heather slopes; grassy gulleys opening on glimmering lochs like tiny oceans, with rocky headlands and bays and solitary trees; near crests against the sky and far away suave outlines; life starting away from the feet, mosses, a strange flower, a bird that disappears before one quite sees it, a peace that until this very moment was unimaginable; a remoteness, a wildness, a curious watching quality inspiring something akin to fear, a nameless primeval fear; a dreariness, a tiredness of the flesh, a tiredness through which one walks into a renewed freshness, when the body seems to gather a second youth; until the point comes where the old existence falls away, leaving little more behind than a half-wondering smile—and the knowledge that perhaps life has other values than those of self-importance and propaganda and the scream of the hurly-burly. Even that "perhaps" is a deceit. One *knows* beyond any doubt—but not aggressively. That ultimate sort of knowledge rarely is aggressive.

And so you get back to your house, or your hotel, or your car.

The one thing about the solitariness of the car is that it keeps up the detached mood. But then, of course, as will have been gathered, such a result is not arrived at easily. Hill and loch and sea do not lay themselves out to entertain. Neither does the car. But the technique for the last half-hour we have reduced to a very simple art. While the bed is being made, I bring the kettleful of water. Into two glasses I pour with luck some cordial out of the heather and add a little of the water. Within a sleeping-bag at such a moment tiredness is a benediction. The light is grey. A cigarette is lit. The night is around as we lie back in floated ease and gaze upon its primeval shapes and stillness through the glass. It is a moment when the earth and the divine intermix.

So much for words—and to believe them all might readily lead to dismay or disaster. They say that Beethoven or even Caledonian spirit is an acquired taste. Meanwhile, there is all the West waiting; its sea-inlets, appearing and disappearing, vivid under the sun in blues and greens; its sudden corners; its water lilies on lochans, its black peat, its brown hide; its wind, its old greyness, its tongues of green, its green mountains; its incomparable air, its variety; lonely croft houses; deer and bird-life and salmon.

When you leave Loch Shin (for I have been running ahead of schedule) you come down among hills and pass a shooting-lodge and lochs from which a river meanders. Once, long ago, I did not know it was a sacred river, and looking into one of its small pools I saw a salmon. Let me record that that river is guarded in a way that will astonish any one and drive him hurriedly to contemplate the mountains.

And the particular feature about the mountains in this north-western world is their individuality. Here are a few of them, seen from one place or another, and seen often. The most famous lie south, such as the jagged Quinag and the exceedingly ancient mass of Ben More Assynt, with Canisp and Suilven beyond Inchnadamph. Suilven is a remarkable mountain, and anyone with a taste for geology could spend his few days here in a dream of Lewisian gneiss, Cambrian quartzite, and Torridon sandstone. If Loch Shin is a bare gut, Loch Assynt has six or seven miles of loveliness along the road that runs by its north shore pretty nearly without their match in Britain.

But this is not an essay in praise of obvious and picturesque spots and historical associations. So let it be said briefly that there is a road from Kylescue to Durness that has to be travelled to be believed by a driver who can drive.

Near the head of Loch Laxford there is a good level stance for a car, and climbing of not too strenuous a kind. I have vivid memories of a weird, misty night spent at that spot. The loch itself was alive with salmon, and all over it you could see the silver bodies launch themselves and fall back with loud splashes.

Midges and mosquitoes and even clegs one can do something with, but the plunging sounds of playful salmon pursue more than the flesh. They mock at sleep. They toss it from one plunge to the next. They play water polo with it. And every now and then a twenty-pounder knocks it clean through the roof of the car.

The night with its grey mist that was a fine rain grew more ghostly. It was twelve midnight by the car clock when I decided to turn over in my sleeping-bag, close my ears and smother the last atavistic instinct. I had hardly performed the act when a hand gripped my arm. It was a dramatic moment. In the gloom her face was pale as she whispered, "Look!"

It was the best ghost that I have ever seen for even in that atmosphere it had a true semblance of reality; not at all the white figure of thought or the theatre but brownish as if it were wearing a mackintosh. It stood quite still, about a dozen yards away, against the sea-loch. It actually took me several seconds to realize that it could only be a gamekeeper.

I breathed then, and as the figure soundlessly withdrew behind an old shed, I confess to a feeling of the most pleasurable irony. For, as it happened, I hadn't even a trout rod. I could hardly have been happier if I had landed one of the twenty-pounders and probably fell asleep while still smiling and certainly slept so soundly that I didn't even hear things go plop in the night. But the ghost had so disturbed the gardener that she couldn't sleep and in the morning I was told a tale of a motorbike that had come and gone and of other mysterious movements by those who had obviously kept us under observation all through the night.

The incident, too, had had its perfect overture earlier in the evening. We had climbed on to a high headland for a glimpse of the inlet as it opened to the western sea. It was a strange glimpse. Islands and headlands, grey lines of low rock above bands of dark weed, with the mist softening, smothering, obliterating. Sound had finally died and no living thing moved.

Then against the water, itself grey as the suspended mist, two tiny spars appeared. Astonished by this, we managed to climb a little higher, and presently we were watching a two-masted yacht as it just perceptibly and utterly silently moved over the face of the lost windless inlet. Surely never did vessel appear more ghostly nor wander with such aimlessness. A small boat came away from her and did a slow circle sun-wise. The silence remained absolute and I thought that possibly a shoal of mackerel had appeared and the crew were netting a few for supper. But, later, I changed the name of the fish.

In the next inlet is Loch Inchard with Rhiconich at its head. It is a good sea-fishing loch, and the road to Kinlochbervie skirts it on the north side. A bare world up there, with sandy shores and rolling green slopes.

But let us cut inland from Rhiconich and cross the Gualan moor in order to get back to the spirit of desolation again. And slowly. There is no hurry. We may as well have the feeling of being lost utterly, were it only to get through it and come out at the other side. In the disputation of our days we so often come out by the same door where in we went. Here we come out at another door, and there is always a sporting chance of our coming out not quite the same—whatever the nature of the change! And so down into Strath Dionard, with two mountains to the right, whose corries I have sometimes seen greener than verdigris. The river runs into the sandy Kyle of Durness; the land opens and lightens; the sea again, the northern sea, far to the Arctic. Cape Wrath is in the offing.

Durness has its features, like the celebrated Smoo Cave of which Sir Walter Scott wrote, or Balnakill with its old ruined church dating from 1619. In the churchyard Rob Donn lies buried, and I know a man who once "rose" from the poet's grave in a white shirt and sonorous Gaelic, calling down doom upon certain worthy if sceptical gentlemen whose quaking legs just managed to take them hurriedly through the gloom of the night from the "haunted" spot. Rob was a skilled poet and a fine poet, with a turn for satire that was swift and penetrating.

That he could neither read nor write never fails to astonish the southern tourist. How many of our poets, rhyming or rhyme-less, would have sung their ingenious lays without pen and paper? It's a thought!

And then there is Balnakill Bay and its wide sands where we stop until we can stop no longer.

And so to a road that encircles both Ben Hope and Ben Laoghal. Let us press by the bleak slopes of Loch Eriboll, where so many fishing-boat skippers I know—or have known, for the days of sail are gone—have lain, waiting for weather to get round the Cape, and let us come in at the tail end of Loch Hope with its lodge and its pines. In front the road winds steeply up to a great tableland of moor (A' Mhoine) from which that whole northern world may be seen in its strength and grandeur, with the granite peaks of Ben Laoghal in the distance looking like battlements of an unearthly castle. But not so fast. We could turn back and take the inland road to Altnaharra, that winds by Loch Hope side, on under the shadows of Ben Hope itself (3,040 feet) and up into the green valley of Strathmore, that knew the bitter tragedy of the clearances. If the vanished races of the clearances are not old enough for fancy, what about the vanished races of the broch, Dun Dornaigil? And the waterfall of Alltnacaillich is there to ponder by.

From Altnaharra, a road goes back to the northern sea by the western side of Loch Laoghal, under the slopes of the classic mountain, and comes out at Tongue, with its surprising woods. Farther east, and almost parallel, a road runs down the strath of the Naver to Bettyhill. Strath Naver of sad memories, but with the salmon of wisdom still coming up from the sea.

I am tempted to recall a night and a morning, and a wild race from midges and other things that stir in the night, but must content myself with saying that no man has ever tasted salmon who, with the hunger on him, has not fried a cutlet for himself while the flesh is still so fresh that it breaks in curd.

174

Take the Hill Path

He was recovering from his illness and, still in bed, roared with laughter when I showed him my catch. He could not believe it was seriously meant. Eleven of them in a row on the tray and the heaviest was three ounces. Three hours they had taken me to catch; and then I told him, quite truly, of the monster I had lost. If he was one pennyweight, I declared, he was all of four ounces.

The laughter did him good; the same kind of good, I suspect, as the outing had done me. For we had mostly fished for salmon together and had memories of outstanding days. Indeed, the last fish I had landed in his company (on the Thurso, just above Halkirk bridge) had weighed 32 lb.

There is a big drop from 32 lb. to 2 oz., but as we now happily know from the scientists, everything in this life is relative, and, measured in terms of excitement against the hunter's world, the difference is no matter.

.   .   .   .   .   .

For it was a wonderful world to look upon. The small hill burn wound round the base of a mountain, and remoteness was in its aspect. Sun on the face and a soft cool wind on the skin, eddying fragrance from heather, from patches of bog myrtle, clean light, mountains, white clouds against blue.

But let us say here and now that the utmost one can do with a feeling is to experience it. The experience is the thing, not any analysis of it. Analysis can strangle it with a piece of string and a label, but that's quite another kind of performance; and as we generally borrow the string and the label, it means for the most part just nothing.

Quite simply we *know* when an experience is pleasant and health-giving and when it isn't. The rest we can leave to those who will debate and quarrel about it for centuries in a very marvellous way. But the individual doesn't live for centuries. In this age he is lucky if he finds himself alive for one blessed day.

So let us see if there is a practical way of holding on to the blessed day—a working technique for this particular day anyhow.

To begin with, there is the immense difficulty of "getting back", of getting into complete accord with the environment. Here the inertia piled up over a long time can be terrific. It's no good saying brightly, "Who would believe that the town is only three miles away?" or "I hope it won't rain." The town has to be forgotten, and the rain, and everything, in fact, except what the eye immediately rests on. If there are whin bushes in bloom—and when are they not in bloom somewhere?—the blossom will have its moment. Or if wild roses, then look at the gradations of pink between the bud and the full-blown flower. Is the brier scent there? Very faintly. What is there in the tang of brier that evokes—what? A haunting scent, this. And the flat-open roses, grown pale in their strange still eagerness, are like faces. You look away and look back. You become half-aware that you are seeing their ardent faces in their own quiet place. They remain there, and you move on. . . . Something caught you that time, and the inertia has perceptibly lightened. The eye is beginning to look more naturally, less self-consciously.

At any time of the year, there is abundance to see. But each thing has to be seen individually. *One thing at a time.* Here is some stag's moss, pushing through the old heather like green adders. Curious sort of stuff. And now it's sending up spears like hackles. Some are two-pronged, some three-pronged, like miniature salmon spears from an older age. Plenty of moss here, too, and coloured lichens, with red spots like shining beetles. You poke your fingers in and about, feel the softness, the ferny damp. No need to be an expert in wild flowers and mosses. Doesn't matter if the names or labels are missing. Here are the things themselves, and if the eye is catching them for the first time, let the eye have its astonished way. And the fingers, too. The sense of touch. When an old cock grouse gets up beside you, your ears are brought in also over a flurry of the heart. I have never known him fail to bring that flurry to the heart. For one instant it is the wild itself coming rocketing alive, and the moor tilts. Last spring a hen grouse sat so close that I all but trod on her. Her wings in my face, the heart in my mouth, and nine eggs at my feet.

That gives old time a bit of a jolt, not to mention the inertia. The shoulders loosen. A keener vision comes of itself to the eye. The feet step more lightly—they had better! The body begins to carry itself. The tiredness of the first uphill mile, the general weariness, is being sloughed off. Adders get out of their old skins regularly. It's beginning to feel pretty good. And behold, there—the first glimpse of the burn.

At first I decided they were too quick for me. I had the very finest tackle, carrying two flies. But after a time I removed one, so that the issue would be dead straight, with no room for excuses. But whether I struck with swiftness or perceptibly delayed, the result was the same. And no trout ever rose twice. The wind was difficult, I admit, and the trout for me uniquely small. The only thing I was sure of was my stalking, for in each partial arrestment of water (one could hardly talk of pools—not to begin with, anyhow) I brought a brown glisten to the top. Then, without striking at all, I caught two in succession.

At last I had solved the problem! The two-ouncer like the thirty-two-pounder preferred to hook himself. Extremes meet. I was triumphant—and in due course proved quite wrong. Three other theories I developed with about equal lack of success, until finally I brought matters to so nice a pass that I became certain the only way to do the trick was to strike before the trout rose. In other words, strike at nothing and there would be an even chance of the trout being there. I admit this was getting perilously near the region of metaphysics. But things can develop oddly enough on this sort of outing. Even metaphysics gets a new twist where all is glisten and shine and quickness, the gush of water, of falling water—on to which I sidestepped by mistake. That was when I lost the four-ouncer.

A hill burn under a summer sky grows fairly warm, but in the first contact with it there is a delicious breath-taking chill. The best thing to do then is shout. In this way you learn why the old cock grouse shouts when he is taken by surprise. There are those who think that intuition works on nothing. Nothing could be further from reality. You will shout in any case—and then you can add an extra yell or two, as the grouse does for the benefit of his mate and family. Possibly he merely flatters himself he is adding them for their benefit. And why wouldn't he?

Suddenly you realize that the sun has skipped a section of the sky; either that or somewhere you must have lost two to three hours of mortal time.

And, more astonishing still, you feel the richer for this wanton extravagance—this extravagance from life's deeper wealth, where the balance sheet is not on paper and the profit knows no income tax. The eleven trout—you fry them quite stiff, and their flavour is delicate. If you can add one rasher of bacon from the ration and some mashed potatoes, you have given yourself, and almost saved your country, a meal. Finally, if extravagance now appeals, you are happily free on the way home to laugh at the thought of how the fellow in bed is going to laugh at you.

A Rabbit in a Snare

We had come round the corner of the small pine wood when we saw the rabbit jumping frantically in the snare. It was the late evening, and the strong blustering rain showers of the day had passed away into that quietude which seems to hold more than rest.

The rabbit must have come out from the warren in the wood for its evening feed, and the sound of our approaching footsteps on the grass had probably sent it into the snare. For rabbits have a strong sense of hearing. I had tested this in the wood itself a month or two ago. I had been sitting on a fallen pine log, with branches overhead and juniper bushes around, when a rabbit hopped into the small clearing. It was a windy day and the thresh of the branches was like the sound of the sea on a beach. I was completely visible to the rabbit and within ten yards of it. For perhaps half a minute it looked at me; then it began eating, hopping and eating. I watched it for a time, greatly taken with the delicacy of its nibbling, the soft brightness of its eye, the incredible cleanness of its fur, so that altogether it was a very special and fastidious creation of the wood. At such a moment it is easy for the imagination to take the next small step into fantasy, though not so easy to discover just why the mind should work so, with such irrational delight. No analysis that I have read of magic by any psychologist, including Freud, ever gets at this quality of delight, and certainly never evokes or transmits it.

I now found that if I made slow movements with my head or with a hand the rabbit did tend to stop to observe them, but on the whole was not much disturbed and in a moment or so was eating again. But when I made a short sharp hiss through my teeth, a sound that I could just hear in my own ears and that a yard or two from my mouth was surely lost in the hissing of the flailing trees, the rabbit instantly had a single convulsive spasm as if physically hit. Indeed so instantaneous appeared to be the reaction that, short as the distance was between us, I could hardly believe the sound had had time to travel across it.

But though the rabbit crouched and kept an eye on me it did not go away, and after a few seconds it raised its head and hearkened to the whole wood; then, tentatively, it started eating again. I repeated this sound, trying to diminish it still further, with the same result. In the end, when I slowly stood up, the rabbit plainly could not believe in me, and only when I took a step forward did it gather its wits and clear off as if death were at its heels.

So our footsteps on the grass must have carried their message to the rabbit round the corner of the wood, and when we came in sight of it, there it was jumping frantically in the snare.

Instinctively we hurried towards it and my friend got down on his knees and caught it. At once the rabbit began squealing. It is not a pleasant sound, and the urge rises instantly to kill the rabbit and so kill the sound. But the rabbit remained very much alive and—what to do about it? "Be quiet!" he said to the rabbit strongly, and started stroking its back. And all at once the rabbit was quiet.

"What'll I do with it?"

"It's the trapper's snare," I said.

The trapper paid a rent for the trapping. The rabbit was his property.

My friend looked around him. There was no one to be seen. "Damn it all!" he said, getting a trifle red in the face from stooping in his close-fitting khaki tunic and from his thought, for the rabbit now lay quiet, with flattened ears, between his hands.

He obviously could not ask me to kill the rabbit. The problem was his own. All at once the rabbit, as he shifted on his knees, leapt from his hands, and in the moment of struggle that followed he very nearly hit it to finish it off. But here it was again in his hands and his fingers were feeling for the wire. And now the way the wire had sunk out of sight through the fur and tightly round the neck claimed his attention. As a first step, he concentrated on getting the wire off the neck. This was something that had to be done anyway. As the rabbit squealed, his fingers fumbled a bit, but they stuck to their business, and presently the golden noose was eased and slipped over the head.

"It seems to be none the worse," he said, and looked at me with a troubled and half-guilty smile. Then he looked at the rabbit. All at once he eased his grip on the rabbit, not quite with the intention of letting it go, but, as it were, to see what would happen. Nothing happened. The rabbit crouched. "It's absolutely terrified," he said, lifting his face again. And at that movement the rabbit leapt and instantly was beyond his thrust and making for the wood.

"I suppose," said my friend, with a somewhat shamefaced glance as he slowly got up, "that was a bit sentimental."

"You certainly have interfered with the trapper's livelihood," I suggested.

"And the country's food supplies."

"Not to mention the damage the rabbits do to the turnips."

All the same, I could see he was more affected than he might care to let appear.

"My only excuse is that it's not often I do a thing like that," he said, wiping his hands. "So why not?"

"You suggest someone has to do the irrational thing occasionally?"

"Well, hasn't one?"

But his conscience was not altogether clear, for about his last remark was, "If I saw the trapper I could give him a couple of bob".

"... Land and Sea, Twin Halves of the Mystery"

One of the more curious results of modern war is the casualty list amid place names. In truth, it is when a place is thriving in an abnormal fashion that its name must not be mentioned in print. My surprise was complete when we dropped into a little port and found drifters and gulls and lorries clustering round its pier which I had expected to find desolate. It was blowing hard, with drenching rain-showers that had the sting of sleet, yet I stood for two hours in the shelter of a hut, cold but fascinated. There is an extraordinary exhilaration in this traffic with the sea. The drifters that had come in early had been lightly fished, and the price had reached the maximum control level, so that the total had been rationed in five-cran lots among the buyers; but now, approaching midday, shots are getting heavier, and bidding stops short of the maximum. As each drifter comes round the point, our interest is once more quickened.

And how proudly each comes, tossing up the spray, taking

the wide sweep, slackening speed, and then slowly nosing up to find a way through the cluster to a landing berth. Let her be however old and rusty and dirty, she never loses this sure grace of movement, this indomitable lift of the bow, this pride of the sea. Nothing that man has ever made so surely touches his heart as this creation of power, courage, and grace, all three in one, moving over deep waters. It was something for man to have done, even should his race now die.

Perhaps there is something more than pride here, too; for history does show that the most repressive forms of tyranny and authoritarian bureaucracy have always been characteristic of great land empires. Not to create but to fix, not to aspire but to ritualize, not to act in individual fullness but to move in mass. Contrast, in old days, the Persians and the Greeks.

About this traffic of the sea there is also that strangely exciting element called luck. Here is a drifter just berthing. The skipper says in his quiet seaman's way that he has about sixty crans. "Good, though!" says a man beside me. We fall into talk and he explains that this particular drifter has been out of luck. Week after week she has been shot just on the outskirts of the shoal, never near the centre. Two or three crans to keep her going; no more. Now her luck has turned; or, at least, her bad luck has been broken. Good for her!

But the top shot of the day arrives with a great colony of gulls. The nets in the hold are a mass of herring. She is an old boat that would have been lying rotting in some inner basin but for the war, which commandeered the best boats. In fact nearly all the drifters here are old and would normally have been laid up. Old, and many of them laden with debt, and done. And they have come back, like some of their old skippers, to take a chance in time of trouble. We speculate, we wait—until the skipper answers someone casually on the pier to the effect that he has about a hundred and fifty crans.

"You can take it he has that anyway," says the man beside

me, and we smile, for the old boy is not likely to overestimate lest so great a weight of fish might be considered to bear rather heavily upon those beneath. Somewhere between one hundred and two hundred thousand herrings in his hold—a fair-sized breakfast, even enough to cover a few large factories!

In due course a sample of the catch is brought to the lee of the shed and the auctioneer mounts the wooden step. "Who'll start me at eighty?" No one will start him at eighty shillings a cran. The skipper is standing a little apart, near the edge of a small crowd, a drop to his nose and a slight pleasant smile on his lined weathered face. The hair beneath his cap is grey and close-cropped. He is not directly interested, it would appear, and quietly answers a man who offers him a cigarette. A soft Buchan voice. The shillings mount—"Eighty I am bid, I am bid eighty, eighty——" I cannot help watching the skipper's face. Its calm pleasant expression never alters. At eighty-two bidding ceases—but starts again, and finally stops at eighty-eight. As if that were another little task over, the skipper goes back to his boat where the crew are shaking the herrings out of the nets. A fresh blatter of rain sweeps the pier in a fierce drenching gust. He steps on board as if the sun were shining.

The man beside me doubts if they will be able to face it to-night. "There are herring on the ground," I answer him. We smile again. And sure enough as, some time later, I leave that little port, I see them putting out, taking it head on, with thin curtains rising from the bows. It will be pretty dirty outside. Again, of course, it may take off a bit. But one look at the boats shows they are not arguing; they are eager, stems lifting, bows to the horizon, indomitable.

I think it is good for a landsman to come in contact with the sea occasionally. Even if he dislikes it, hates it, it will all the more certainly quicken his affection for the land. He will return to his farmyard, to his fields, to his cornstacks, with cleansed eyes and see them as a blessing of rich quietude. They are solid.

The stacks are a deep gold; they are bursting with food. The old land, bright with the sad lovely pageantry of autumn, is stable under his feet.

It is this quickening of affection that the ever-increasing mechanization of life over recent years has tended to weaken. Perhaps all our ills and tragedies could be traced, were the eyes of our understanding clairvoyant enough, to interference with the expression of some simple natural emotion, such as affection.

At any rate, it may be worth a few argumentative words. For example, a full stackyard may mean to the farmer's eye a calculable sum of money. This indeed to him is the ultimate reality of the stackyard. We see his point of view, recognize that it is eminently practical, and agree that this man knows his business. At any other point of view, if he has the patience to listen to it, he may smile tolerantly. Yet it is none the less a fact that by seeing in the stackyard a bank balance, he is performing a mental trick, he is equating the stackyard's reality in terms of something else.

Quite simply, its ultimate reality is not a bank balance but life itself. Forget that and the argument will draw us farther and farther away from the clear-seeing eye and the quick movement of affection, from the stacks of grain that mean man's traffic with the earth, as a boat his traffic with the sea, and as both mean the abundance of life, this mysterious warm thing that stays with us for a short time, we know neither why nor whence, that is moved by the autumn colours and the shape of a cornstack and the lifting prow of a boat. Translate it into anything other than itself and at that moment death knocks at the door.

My arm was caught by the gardener. With mounting alarm, I reached the end of the rockery. A finger pointed: "At last!"

For three years she has had great difficulty in keeping alive a small root of autumn gentian given by a friend now dead. There, before us, five blue trumpets lifted to the sun. The blue was very beautiful.

The Keeper in War-time

I have been in the woods and on the hill once or twice with a gamekeeper. Such outings in these busy days are rare, and a keeper's job is not what it was. As we ate our simple lunch in a sheltered spot, he began talking of shooting in "the old days", of the dogs, the restricted number of guns, the almost rigid etiquette of a sporting system that seemed destined to last for his time, if not indeed for ever. He shook his head. "It's on its last legs," he said, "and going fast."

He was full of old experiences, some of them very entertaining, with an eye for personal idiosyncrasy that would have astonished him whom it concerned, but always with that breadth of view and tolerance which contact with nature in all her moods tends to breed. "He was a tyrant, but he was fair, too. I'll say that for him. When he got in a rage, I just let him curse away." Or "Mr. ——, ah, he was a gentleman if ever there was one, and a first-class shot! I remember once, a frosty forenoon it was after a full moon that had brought the woodcock in . . ."

That leisured world, with its privilege, its town and country seasons, came alive again, and it seemed, as we sat there still requiring four pairs of rabbits to fill his hamper, like recalling a period play.

The younger keepers and gillies were in the army.

The war has dealt more hardly with the older men—particularly with deer stalkers beyond military age, many of whom served in the first world war and are now looking for a job. They know only their own job, to which they have given all their lives. In one forest, which has been let on lease and therefore surely secure as far as rental is concerned, the head-stalker, whom I knew well, has been informed that his wages are to cease—though he may live on in his house if he likes, and even take a few sheep to graze. Sheep, deer, and the Highland chief. There is room for sardonic reflection on the fate of this head-stalker and clansman who has spent a lifetime in the service of his chief, a lord of many mountain ranges.

This morning when we had started at the first warren and had discovered that for some reason it was not going to be a good day for rabbits bolting, I had heard beyond the tree-tops a high crying in the air.

"What is it?" I asked.

"A hawk—crying for his mate, likely."

Everywhere the enemies of the wild game were increasing, hawks, foxes, wild cats.

But what can one old keeper do to keep a whole sporting estate in condition? Not a great deal, even if he could give all his time to it. But here now was my friend devoting his days to rabbit shooting and trapping.

Hampers had to be filled and dispatched. Prices were high—and the estate was poor. A fairly common story now. And it is not likely that estate owners will become richer in any discernible future.

A cold but pleasant sunny morning there in the wood, with the warrens round and about the great roots of smooth-boled beeches. I hadn't seen a ferret at work for years. One was mature and well trained, but the young fellow was all wild life together and remarkably swift with his bite. He had to be handled with quick, firm assurance. The pink eyes in the sniffing, sensitive face, the undulating flow of the white body, the snap of the teeth that did not let go. Delicate, exotic-looking beasts in that setting, and only now and then did you get a glimpse of their ruthless pursuit.

When Sandy, the mature one, was dropped into a burrow, young Jock kept the small canvas sack, in which he was tied, thrusting about like a burst football gone demented. Never for an instant was it still. More than once the sack had to be pulled back from the mouth of a burrow, towards which, over an extremely erratic yard, he had somersaulted and generally performed his interior acrobatics.

It is the only moving object in our waiting world. So it is going to be a day like that! We glance at the sky, consider the weather, and wonder once more what mysterious influence makes rabbits bolt freely one day and very reluctantly, if at all, another. Plainly Sandy has got stuck. The keeper is disappointed. "It's not like him," he mutters. It all has happened before, exactly in the same way.

Flat on the ground with an ear in a burrow we listen. No sound. We get sticks and whack the ground. Nothing happens. At long last we gather dried beech leaves and set them alight in the mouth of a burrow in order to smoke Sandy out. As the keeper fans the flame with his cap the smoke spreads and the ancient scent of wood fire comes upon the nostrils. What is it in this scent that stirs the mind with so curious a pleasure? As I am bringing up more leaves, two rabbits bolt in a complete get-away. It is the sort of thing that happens. We are in the world of nature and the wild knows us.

Still Sandy does not appear, though smoke is now showing at various openings. The keeper releases young Jock. He may shift him! As Jock is just about to disappear, I let out a shout. Swiftly the keeper catches Jock by the tail, lifts him up against his knee, grabs him under the forelegs, and returns him to his bag. Sandy has emerged, and is sniffing the aromatic world with delicate nostrils.

At the next burrow I catch glimpses of a remorseless hunt by Sandy. The rabbit refuses to leave the network of burrows, made very intricate by the thick roots of a beech, and every now and then appears for a moment, closely pursued by that lithe white body.

The keeper is standing on top of the warren, waiting for Sandy. All at once a rabbit comes out and sits beyond the mouth of the burrow looking at the keeper, who remains as still as the tree trunk. Its ears are down, its eyes bewildered and soft. But clearly, after all, there is little danger out here. It hops past the keeper's feet, going, as it were, quietly. As the keeper moves, it bolts.

It is a remarkable fact that among hunters and fishermen you discover human nature at its finest and kindest. Rarely do you ever find it warped and never caught up in that "idealism" which is capable of so fiendish a cruelty that it would annihilate half the human species to achieve its end or—if there is any difference—glut its lust for power.

Another morning we set off for some low hills to see if there were any woodcock about. The keeper was also concerned about hiding bundles of rabbit traps here and there for work in the next few days. I asked him if he cared for the trapping. "Ach, well," he said, "it's all in the day's work, and perhaps in my small way I'm helping to feed the country!" He smiled as he went on at an even climbing pace that soon had the sweat on my forehead. But he could not climb as he used to, he said, because he was gassed in the last war and still felt the effects of it.

Then we had an experience that brought the present war very near to us. We had been beating along a hillside of withered bracken and small bushes, the dog working between us, when the keeper, who was above, came to a small ridge and was stopped by a wild shout just beyond him. From my position I could not see who had shouted. The keeper turned smartly back and flagged me down, crying at the same time, "A bomb!"

I glanced around for shelter, but there was none, so I flopped where I was. Seconds passed—perhaps ten—and then there was such a terrific explosion that it was heard miles away. One stone came down about a yard from my head and buried itself out of sight in the turf. Others thudded into the earth around. There were a few lively seconds before the keeper at last got up.

I joined him as we slanted towards the pine wood. Figures in battledress were clearly testing some engine of war. We naturally did not ask questions, and they could certainly be pardoned for not expecting human intruders in that lonely spot. It was as well, however, that I had not gone a yard farther before flopping. What is it, this queer thing we call luck? And why do we stretch out to touch wood at even mentioning the word? In the old days when fishermen set out for the perils of the sea in their open boats folk did not wish them luck. It is unwise to let the dark ones hear too much. When things were going too well with the ancient Greeks did they not throw away some valuable possession?

It was peaceful up in the pine wood, with a trickle of water singing its small song, mossy banks brown with needles, a blue sky with its slow-moving herd of clouds, cold shadows among the trees, and sun warmth in the clearing.

Pigeons would come in here in the late afternoon; a covey of partridge would be down in the low stubble field, and perhaps a cock pheasant in the turnips. The freshness and optimism of this clear winter's day are in the mind. We are in no hurry to finish lunch.

And perhaps, after all, a new order of gamekeeping will arise. Why should not a gamekeeper be a responsible servant of the community, skilled in the knowledge of wild life, in wood-craft and hillcraft? Not a slayer of rabbits in mass, but a wise preserver and administrator to whom those who love the wilds could go for instruction and refreshment—on the actual hill, or on a well-stocked loch for which there would be a permit at a price.

At any rate, the talk was pleasant enough to moisten the sand-wiches, after the burn water and the flask had been introduced.

A Blank Day

Many have been astonished—and deceived—by the way a mother bird will trail an apparently broken wing in an effort to draw away attention from her young, but I had not experienced deception of the kind among the animals of the wild.

The stalk had been quite a simple one, and when the man with the rifle slowly turned his head over his shoulder and nodded to me, I carefully crawled to the heather ridge and saw the hind well under two hundred yards away standing in a fairly extensive bed of rushes. We had been discussing the merits of venison on the way to the hill, of yeld hinds and young stags, for warriors were coming on leave and something was needed for the pot. Anyway, there was the hind in the thick rushes and whether she was a yeld beast or not I could not say, though she certainly looked reddish-brown. But my friend drew his rifle up, poked it through the heather ridge and took aim.

It was my clear impression that he missed. The hind started forward uncertainly, glancing around for the danger point. There was the click of the bolt as a new cartridge went home, then raising himself slightly my friend fired again. Now, on his knees, he cried that he had hit her. And it did indeed look as if he were right for the hind, after prancing a few paces to one side, suddenly flopped and was hidden by the rushes. She had seen us, of course, perfectly clearly and would have been bounding away at top speed had she not been knocked out.

"It's often like that," said my friend as we approached the rushes. "One day you have hardly entered the hill when you get your beast. The next time you'll go all day and, from one bit of bad luck to another, you'll never get a shot."

At that moment, not more than fifteen yards in front of us, the hind leapt to her feet and cleared off at uninjured speed, closely followed by a calf. We just stood and gaped at them until they had disappeared.

Stalking is a true art, and we had some splendid stalks that day. Away in the heart of the forest is another world. The moor, the corrie, the line of distant tops and ridges against a clear blue sky. The spaciousness into which the eyes roam. The loneliness that is a rare companionship. The tough hill grass, indescribably beautiful in the play of the strong wind. The colour of a golden sherry it was, and the wind raced over it in undulations and eddies, caressingly or in wild frolic, over whole square miles of it, as if it were the hide of a golden beast, this hide of the old earth.

Fifteen yards from the shallow ridge I raised my head slowly, with the utmost care. I lay flat again and nodded. They were still there, a whole small herd of them. We wiped the sweat from our foreheads and took a breath or two; then forward once more, flat to the earth. Heavy work it had been over the last hundred yards and my heart was certainly pounding. But

only twenty more yards. Carefully now, remembering to keep
the stern down as well as the head. Very carefully—now——

They were gone! The whole moor in front of us was vacant.
I could not believe it, as if the deer had vanished by a particularly incredible sort of magic. I felt the necessity to justify myself by assuring my companion that I really had seen the deer.
They had been eating, not at all disturbed. They could not have
spotted me. Which was certainly true. But manifestly some
outlying beast, which I had not seen, had seen me. Going forward, we picked up their tracks and shortly thereafter, far away
on the low slopes of a hill, we saw them proceeding at a walking
pace in a long file. To me there is always something strangely
attractive in this distant vision of deer trekking in a drawn-out
line. Whether the mind, on its own, draws fantastic analogies
with eastern caravans or rakes up some dim ancestral memories,
I am sure I don't know.

We started on our long and intricate new stalk. All went well
until we came to the inevitable place where we could go no
farther without exposing ourselves along a piece of flat ground
there was no possible circumventing. We rested, of course, and
had our strategic talk—to me always a delightful interlude. At
that moment the whole stalk is held in poise. Something has
been accomplished, but the real difficulty lies ahead, so that
keenness is not only sustained but sharpened, while yet the body
lies back and takes its ease and the eyes have a small wandering
holiday on their own. Then one more look—at the heads of the
two beasts which are lying down on guard. They are staring
down the long slope of the hillside straight at us. I give it as my
opinion that if we crawl slowly, pausing now and then but not
looking up, we shall almost certainly succeed. We were both in
brown tweeds.

There was never any difficulty and clearly no slightest sus-
picion travelled upward. We now had about a mile's trek under
tufted hags and up a small water course. It was when we began

to draw in on them again from the right that I found how far out I was in my private estimate of where the beasts should be. But my companion, who knew his forest, never hesitated, even if he did make the mistake of beginning to come in too low so that we had to back away again.

The last part of the stalk was very simple, and after trying the wind with a wisp of dry grass, we saw that we need have no real fear of their getting our scent on any sort of eddy.

It was too simple. My companion slowly lifted his head, paused, and as slowly drew it down again. He beckoned me to follow his example. When I caught the tips of antlers on the other side of the knoll less than twenty yards from us, I, too, subsided. We smiled, in our dilemma. The brute was too near us!

What to do now? He suggested the only course, but when, the rifle in front of him, he raised his head, the stag was already tentatively on the move. He now made his mistake, for he showed himself, anxious to get a shot. If only he had lain low, and crawled a yard or two he could have had his pick of a number of beasts, because, though disturbed, it was presently clear that they had not made up their minds about the real danger spot. They escaped and no damage was done.

Now a very interesting point arose here, because it was dead certain that the stag had neither seen us nor winded us. The stalker said, "We were so near him he sensed our presence."

There is one other theory I tentatively put forward. I had noticed on one part of the moor, which was a bit wet and boggy, that I clearly felt a trembling or quake in the ground from the treading of my friend's feet many yards away. Here on the firm hillside I would have felt nothing, and we certainly had been moving with great care. But it is just possible that to the delicate senses of the stag some perceptible tremor was conveyed, sufficient to make him vaguely uneasy.

Yet I like that idea of his "sensing" our presence. I have

heard a woman say, "I felt someone was in the room." The same idea; and in such matters a deer may be much more sensitive than a woman, for the deer's life more often depends on what it "feels" in this fashion.

The final stalk of the day had one interesting feature. When at long last we came to the ridge and poked our eyebrows up, I was dismayed to find that the herd which should have been less than two hundred yards away had completely vanished. But my friend whispered, "They're all lying down," and then he tried to indicate the spot where one head was manifestly visible to him. But try as I would I could not pick it up in that broken ground. "They're all there", he whispered, noiselessly sliding home the bolt of the rifle and laying the weapon in front of me. After his failures, he insisted that I should shoot, so I got into position.

His piercing whistle brought the ground alive with deer in what seemed really a miraculous manner. They trotted on to a small ridge and paused, broadside on, in perfect silhouette. Never could a man hope for a better shot. I knew the rifle well, knew I could hardly miss hitting the beast I had selected, and steadied grimly to make it a fatal shot. I completed the pressure on the trigger. Nothing happened. I pulled and pulled again. Nothing happened. The deer began to move away; broke into a run. My friend, in shoving the cartridge in, had for once in his life not brought the bolt far enough back to make the trigger alive.

So it was the deer's day off, and for me, gratefully, a day of fresh wind and golden moor and memorable stalks. As for the pot—why, to-morrow is always another day.

Violets and Red Berries

Going up the hill-road this afternoon, I passed three teams ploughing, followed by gulls. The black earth gleamed in the furrow, the horses' heads bent to the powerful shoulders that took the strain, the ploughmen were warm at their peaceful task.

Then I came to the tractor, bogging itself in the soft ground of the steep hillside, retreating, bogging itself again, and next time, with an extra roar, getting off and away. The driver was glad of a chat in order to warm his hands and get some feeling back into his feet which were "like lumps of lead". In ordinary circumstances, dragging his triple ploughshare, he would turn over more than the combined efforts of the three teams of horses. But these wheels! He shook his head. "I understood when I fee'd that I was to get caterpillars," he said. With a caterpillar tractor "I wouldn't have thanked it".

There are many ideals. But the work goes on. So long as man looks after the soil decently, recognizing that it, like himself, can become exhausted, ploughs and sows and reaps, the harvest is assured. In the heart of chaos, this alone at times seems the only certainty.

Yet beneath and around this containing structure of life how forgetful we tend to become of the detail that civilizes it! How much is offered "on the side" that a man would not even notice were it not brought right under his nose!

Take so simple a matter, for example, as rock violets. They grow readily in great clumps and come up year after year. The gardener gives them special attention in her rockery. She recalls the vases of tall flowers which in city restaurants served the function of obscuring the faces of our friends. "Would you mind, miss," we said, "removing these?"

Now the gardener has cut-crystal vases only some three inches high, but shapely and pleasant to the eye. Filled with a small bunch of these rock violets, they can stand unobtrusively between what's left of the margarine and the empty sugar-basin. An egg in the egg-cup would almost out-top them. You can lift the vase between thumb and forefinger and sniff it just as you might the egg. Only, you can rely on the violets.

For their fragrance is delicate, a little elusive in cold weather but always holding the memory of wild honey; their purple-blue deepens in shadow to velvety depths where petal outline is lost in a profound glow of violet.

Further, they are not an affair of a brief season, like the wild rose. They have been in constant bloom with us from March until November. Eight months of loveliness. I understand that only one main precaution has to be taken; it is a very simple one: nip off the old blooms when you see them begin to fade.

Again, take the wild rose, or at least its berries. Many towns-folk were astonished recently to learn by radio not only that the hip was edible, but also that it contained a respectable vitamin (or were there more than one?). A city man told me recently that as a boy on his memorable jaunts into the country he was warned by his parents against the hip as a poisonous berry.

As country boys we knew this fruit in all its different flavours, from the crisp appley taste (the best) to the soft and cheesy, and could differentiate with a glance. We broke the berry in half, scooped out the seeds with the thumb-nail, then with a puff of breath blew away what soft fluffy stuff remained and popped it into the mouth.

I have known various names for the hip and recently in Ross-shire heard it called "muckack" and in Caithness "muckie-farlie". That last name has surely some soft characteristic of the berry in it.

People sometimes wonder how the Highlands in the old days bred such a hefty race of men on so limited a variety of food; and, more particularly, seeing they did not go in for vegetable growing to any extent, how they managed a balanced diet containing all the now famous and indispensable vitamins.

But that curious word "muckiefarlie" has already evoked memories and now a whole range of eating stuffs from hazel nuts in the woods to dulse on the seashore crowd upon the mind. Many, like the nuts and the dulse, are universally familiar, but not upon these does the mind linger with a particular pleasure. I had just remembered the old man who told me that in his "young day" they ate primroses, when right on top came a personal boyhood recollection of eating the seeds of the wild violet. We knew the tiny pods as intimately as we knew the hips on the brier. At a glance we could distinguish between "a cock" and "a hen" and on splitting open the two pods were confirmed by the seeds, which looked like tiny seed-pearls and differed slightly in colour.

To suggest that these were eaten out of sheer hunger is wrong. They were just eaten if come upon as a boy nowadays eats a sweet. Boys are great eaters and love to taste queer flavours and unusual things.

But the flesh, fish, and berries of the Highlands are admittedly of so superb a flavour that we need not dwell on them here. For what suddenly arrested the mind was, in modern jargon, "the economy" of a violet. The flower for beauty, the seed for eating, the roots for medicinal purposes and (I am prepared to put my money on this) the plant itself for "a vegetable dye". Surely it need not be surprising that a civilization which could so deal with a wild violet could also set about producing hefty men. To those who know the substance what matters the word —even when it is a word like "vitamins"?

Visitors

Scenes away from home come back to mind of an evening like birds to a tree. From the lee of the bridge, as the deck heaves to the roll in the Minch, I am listening again to an Englishman, in dark blue, telling me what he thinks of the natives of those parts. He is quiet in manner and thoughtful, and what he has to say conjures up moving pictures with that subtle touch of distortion which gives them a fresh, a laughing interest. . . .

Now it is quite dark on board and I am talking to a native, skipper of a minesweeper, going home on sick leave. Two vessels have been sunk under him, blown up. The wind is rising a bit and the night getting very cold. I offer him a cigarette and we light up. Presently there are footsteps coming down from the dark bridge. I cannot see who it is, but the captain's voice says gruffly, "Put out those cigarettes". The Lewisman and myself talk for a long time after that in the black-out. . . .

A crowded train compartment in daylight, including a Lewis girl and a young Welsh sailor. The girl is asked to sing and does so, straight away, as naturally as she would in a *ceilidh* at home, though we are all strangers to one another. Her voice is high-pitched and thin, and I think of sea-birds crying above the waves on the western shore we have left behind. She sings in Gaelic and the effect has a weird necromantic quality. The Welsh sailor sings a sentimental ballad with such rich, swelling, glorious power that the sheer unexpectedness of it moves us to wonder. A middle-aged merry man in his home-going week-end suit says, "I'm a salmon fisher. I canna sing. But I can do the next best thing", and he produces a flat half-bottle of whisky in the sound belief that we are a' Jock Tamson's bairns. . . .

Have you ever approached an old and well-loved place after an absence and found yourself smiling as this feature or the other came in view, really smiling so that you felt it necessary to smooth the smile away at sight of a stranger lest he think you "queer"? If the place is an island and your ship ploughs smoothly through the light on the sea, you can look at it, standing, borne onward on the dreamlike rhythm of the ocean. . . .

Now that the mood has got control scenes from these last months drop in like unexpected friends paying a call.

Death of the Lamb

As he approached the solitary elm in the upland pasture field of the large glen farm, his eye was caught by the flight of a grey crow from its upper branches. His mind quickened sharply for he did not like the bird; his eyes narrowed as they followed the watchful sideways flight, the careless haphazard onflying that was always so sinister; then they dropped to search around and saw the full-grown lamb in the long grass of the ditch.

He came within a few feet of it and stopped. A round hole over two inches deep and about an inch across had been eaten out of its right flank. The hole was red but no blood flowed from it. The lamb swayed very slightly on its legs, its eyes were inclined to close and its ears to droop.

The man was seized with a strong revulsion of feeling, with a hatred of the loathsome grey-black bird, with anger, and also with a desire to walk away, for he could do nothing. There was no-one anywhere to be seen; no-one who had seen him. Even the crow had vanished. He took a few steps downward and paused, for as surely as he went on would the crow return and continue its ghastly meal. The earth around him caught the dark silence of a battlefield.

He went back to the lamb and stared at it, stooped to stare into the red hole, at the intermittent quiver that went over the flesh, at the half-closed eyes, at the head drooping towards fatal

205

sleep. It seemed quite unaware of him. Death wasn't far off—yet the brute was still on its legs, might endure like this for hours, perhaps a whole night, and its eyelids would continue to flicker down to defeat the beak that liked to peck the eyeball as a titbit.

He glanced about the grass, looking for a stone or a stick. There was neither. One sharp blow on the forehead and all would be over. But it was not his lamb. There was nothing he could properly do about it except walk away and report the matter to the shepherd should he happen to come across him. So he set off, leaving the lamb swaying in the tall grass, lifting an eye to watch for the crow, with bitter anger in his mind and a queer undefined hatred. Once he cleared his throat and spat, but that did not cleanse his mouth.

Soon he felt he must find the shepherd, and when he saw the farm workers harvesting a field, he went through the wire fence and strolled over towards them. Yes, there was the shepherd helping with the stooking, and he knew at once a sharp sense of relief. When he had told the shepherd, his responsibility would end.

"Come to give us a hand?" the shepherd greeted him cheerfully.

The man returned the sally and after they had chatted about the good crop said: "By the way, there's a lamb of yours up there on its last legs. A crow was pecking a hole in its flank. It's still standing."

"Oh," said the shepherd, and looked at him.

"I didn't know what to do about it, so thought I'd come and tell you."

"I see," said the shepherd, looking away. Then he picked up a couple of sheaves and set them leaning against each other. "It seems he's done for in that case."

"Yes."

The shepherd picked up another couple of sheaves, and then

paused. There obviously wasn't much that he could do about it. He seemed reluctant to leave the field. "I had one that went like that last week." He walked away a few paces and came back with another two sheaves.

"I felt like putting it out of its misery, but I didn't know what to do, so I thought I'd tell you," said the man, looking at the other workers.

When the shepherd had completed his stook of eight sheaves, he paused again. "Is it far up?"

"Not very. Just up at the elm tree. I don't suppose there's much you can do for it."

"No," said the shepherd in a flat voice; then he began to move over to his black jacket which lay against a stook. When the shepherd had his jacket on, they started walking across to the fence. The shepherd took out his pipe and paused to light its already half-consumed tobacco. "When they get that trouble on them, there's nothing can be done."

He felt that the shepherd now had a grudge against him, and this embarrassed him. There was nothing a man could do. He should have left the shepherd alone, instead of coming like a sensitive woman to tell what he had seen. But he answered in his normal voice, and the shepherd spoke calmly. Yes, there were showers, but the wind soon dried everything up. It was good enough harvest weather.

As they approached the elm-tree, two crows got up and flapped away. "Ugly brutes," said the shepherd, and then, going forward, he stood before the lamb.

It was still on its legs, swaying very slightly, shivering now and then, its eyelids half-closed, its head drooping. The shepherd squatted down and peered at the bloody hole; then remained squatting for a long time, apparently lost in contemplation of the lamb.

He got up with an odd and distant air. In a voice dry and practical, he said: "No, there's nothing can be done now, nothing but the one thing." He looked at the tree and abroad over the bare upland pasture. "You need a licence to kill a beast these days," he said with a humour in which there was no stress. Then he took out his pocket-knife and opened the big blade.

"Well," he greeted the lamb, patting it gently on the back. "It will be all right now, all right." He got his left hand across the throat. The lamb struggled. "It's all right," murmured the shepherd soothingly, "all right", as if talking to a fevered child, and now with all his strength he was getting at the bone. The vertebrae snapped, and the shepherd severed the spinal cord which then showed between the bone joints like two frilled ends of white tape. He dropped the lamb. The body continued to jerk convulsively.

The shepherd cleaned the blade of his knife by stabbing it in the grass. Then he gave it a final wipe against his trousers.

"It's a job I hate," he said in his calm voice as he clicked the blade shut.

"Well, I'm glad it's out of its misery, anyway," said the man as lightly as he could.

They returned, as they had come up, talking in even, friendly tones, but when the shepherd left him the man felt that in some way he had been a soft fool. Also there was somehow in the air a feeling of misery, of guilt. The shadow of the whole business had not only come between the shepherd and himself, but between himself and everything. It attached itself to his clothes and to the trees, and the grey crows flew through it.

Talking of the Weather

The bank had been pressing fishermen to keep up their payments of interest and loan redemption. Then war broke out—and fulfilled the prophecy of the skipper who had told me that it would take a war to raise prices. A decent week at the seine net with a forty-foot boat could now gross £200. High finance! A handful of such weeks and debt may be made to look a trifle silly, and even a skipper may dream of a more powerful engine than the 26 h.p. unit which he knows is not enough and is losing him fish. So the sky is anxiously scanned. What does that cloud "carry" signify? Will it be a sea morning when dawn breaks? The sea rises. Day after day it smashes over the quay-point or harbour wall. Dirty weather has settled in; an anxious man can get the fatal feeling that, after all, there is no reason why it should ever break. I once stood by in an east-coast creek for three weeks in January when the problem was not one of getting to sea but of saving the craft that rode so perilously at their many moorings. From under a leaden sky that lay on the sea, the great waves came pouring, onrushing, mounting, smashing over, hour after hour, day after day, in a breath-choking monotony, dizzying, stupefying, while down over the harbour wall, as the tide rose, the vessels continuously lifted and swung at their moorings, drawing them taut as fiddle strings in the final check that saved them from disaster.

No townsman, not even a crofter or farmer, can understand the meaning of weather in this ultimate sense. I have had enough experience of it to make me think—quite involuntarily and sometimes against my desire—of men and ships at sea, should I happen to be wakened in a warm bed by the roar of the wind. Pictures come willy-nilly. For it is all too easy to visualize the inferno off Cape Wrath or the Butt with the wind in the north; to see the grey sleek craft that, hour after plunging hour, keep their patrol northward towards the Arctic. The radio news has just told us that owing to weather conditions there was no enemy activity over this country last night, nor did our bombers leave their base. I had had a look outside before turning in: a dirty thick night blowing half a gale, bitterly cold, with the wind in the north-east. I once sat on top of a northern lighthouse and watched some minesweepers making round the head. Half the time they were under water. What it was like north of the Shetlands last night in craft with narrow accommodation is not beyond imagining. There are no headlines for these lads, little place in the news, no glamour; but when some of us waken to the howl of the wind in black nights our thoughts are on smashing seas before we can stop them.

Harvesting the Golden Grain

I had driven motor-bikes and motor-cars from an early age and on occasion had even taken the wheel of a cargo vessel, with steering gear worked by steam, under the eye of a pilot who knew the invisible rocks and currents of some of our own western lochs or fiords. And stemming an eight-knot tidal race in Caolas nan Con with the visible rocks so near that you could nearly spit on them can produce a few anxious minutes in an eight-knot vessel. Indeed, when I begin to think of it, I am struck afresh by the degree to which mechanization has invaded the immemorial occupations or handicrafts of man within little more than a generation. As a boy I had been to sea with sailing boats. A marine engine for a fishing boat would in those days have been beyond the dreams of grey-bearded man. Now in the smallest creek a sail is almost a thing of the past, and last year on the shores of Loch Torridon I was told a story by a fisherman which rather aptly sums up the change. This fisherman's grandfather used to go north to Loch Inchard for the herring fishing in an open boat that hadn't even a sail and was pulled the whole eighty or ninety miles by oar. The old man lived long enough to see an aeroplane fly overhead but that did not impress him nearly so much as the small propeller blades in his grandson's large new fishing boat. He would sit on the beach for long spells looking at the blades which were no bigger than his open hands. "He never got over the wonder of it," said his grandson.

But there was one thing I had never done and that was drive an agricultural tractor.

Knocking up or straightening out the ripe grain that wind and rain have flattened and twisted in whorls may look simple enough work, but actually it is both tedious and heavy. I began to envy the lad on the seat of the tractor as it came roaring by. When a driver was needed for a second tractor I willingly volunteered. A couple of minutes were all that were required by way of instruction, and off I set.

There is a feeling of great satisfaction in driving a powerful engine. The horse-power of this one must have been about twenty-six, but being low-geared and fed with paraffin, it seemed much greater. Then again we were working a twenty-five-acre field that was not only on a very considerable slope but in itself waved like the western ocean in smooth hummocks and knolls. Sometimes we were lying over at so steep an angle that the binder which I was pulling behind tended to slip away from the grain. The elderly man who operated the binder was due to let out a shout when anything went wrong with his cutting gear, but as he had rather a wheezy voice and as the exhaust outlet roared in front of my nose, I very soon found out that I could not hear him even when he did his best. Accordingly, I had to steer a very careful and exact course ahead with my head twisted astern, or, at least, I had continuously to be dividing my attention, with the result that on the following day I could look neither one way nor the other without a certain painful effort.

However, I enjoyed driving the tractor. It had one feature that I particularly liked. Its mechanism is unlike a motor-car's in that you do not need to be always operating the throttle. As you approach a steep place and feel you should open out something still further, you merely have to wait for the engine. There is a momentary slackening of speed, then the engine, like a horse getting its shoulders into the collar, opens out of itself. You can feel the extra power being generated under you. There is no back-firing or racing or other skittish performance, only deep undefeatable power being generated by a need of the engine itself. And up she goes, steadily up, eating into the grain, sinking into a rabbit burrow or hummocking over a stone, but up towards the crest and over the crest, and as she roars her relief you throttle her back a little as you might pat a horse after a bit of difficult labour well done.

In these first days of September the weather was glorious, so good indeed that we were out after a break for food at six o'clock and worked until darkness stopped us at nine.

Though there was no darkness really, or at least only the darkness that is lit by a full moon. I have one particularly vivid memory. As I made for that steep crest on the last round, the moon hung above the glen, and as we slowly roared over the crest in deep-powered triumph I lifted my eyes and saw far in the distance the crests of mountain ranges. The golden grain, dark pines towards the moor, and, around the horizon, the mountains of the Highlands. A fine land in which to be reaping the bread of life.

Harvesting is hard work. The casual labourer like myself finds it hard enough in all conscience, but then he may import into it some mood of national necessity or earthy romance or what not. For the regular farm-worker with his long daily hours in all weathers the whole affair of farm labour takes on a different aspect. Forking manure out of a solid heap, hoeing turnips hour after weary hour, handling turnips stiff with frost, ploughing through showers of driving sleet, inhabiting houses with few amenities, little room space, and large families—the average farm-worker has undoubtedly had a tough deal for centuries.

Yet when harvest time comes, always for him this has been

the crown of his year's labours, and he gets down to it with a real zest. His is a hard living, and with the increasing tempo of the work, there may be natural weariness and occasion for real grumbling, but, as though it were the one thing that finally justified his existence, the harvest must be saved.

This year where on some farms four times more grain has been grown than before the war, the work has been quickened and prolonged. Labour is a difficult problem because much farm work—like building a cornstack, for example—is highly skilled. And always at the back of the mind is a consciousness of racing the weather. As good day follows good day men work like those to whom Fate has handed a respite. To get it all in *before* the weather breaks, that would be great luck. It could rain then!

Rain comes, of course. But the glass goes down so quickly that it will start going up again very soon. Thunder in the warm air. Heavy clouds. It clears by midday and here's a drying wind. September is nearly always a good month, folk say. We feel September is a kindly month, full of golden colour, and wonder why more people do not holiday in the Highlands that month. July and August, now—you can get very broken weather then, wet and miserable, and even cold. But September—it is so often a lovely month, warm, and touched with the scents of autumn.

Thus we salute the month, in confidence and optimism, as field after field gathers its stacks of grain in a convenient place. For we no longer think of gathering them all into one mighty stackyard. That would be too great a target for the enemy, too obvious a disposition for the dark gods, the destructive ones. Even the harvested grain we will deploy for our defence.

In the gathering of food, an occasional odd incident happens to relieve the tedium of the workers. One evening, with the moon coming up and labour drawing to a close, I was leaning on my fork talking to an old man when a young lad started leaping in among the standing corn. He had seen a rabbit, and soon the hunt was in full swing, with a collie dog guarding the outfield.

The rabbit cannot run quickly through the corn, and on the sharp stubble left by the binder his speed is greatly reduced. In the gathering gloom, with the running figures and the quick shouts, the doubling rabbit, the mounting excitement, the poised figures as the rabbit is momentarily lost in the corn, the quick eyes, the ears listening for a rustle in the dry grain, the shout and sudden break into action again, the rabbit once more, the doubling rabbit with its ears down—the scene takes on a primordial hunting quality and we inhabit a world before civilization began.

The Fall

This year everyone is happy about the harvest weather. Even the solitary old crofter, who is always behindhand, has in these last days of October got his whole field of oats cut. For a while I doubted if he was going to manage it, for part of the field was still pretty green in mid October, but it is all in stook at last. It may not thresh very well, but for him it will be enough.

Down on the big farms in the glen, the ploughing of the stubble is well forward. The potatoes have been lifted—a bumper crop and of excellent quality. Already a tidy bit of money has been made on this year's crop. One old farmer told me that he cleared, after expenses—and they were heavy—about £40 an acre. He had twelve acres. Hitherto his small farm had been let out to pasture, for his real interests lay outside farming, but what with the adverse effects of the war on his business and the official instruction to plough up all available land, he turned to his first love and is now "making a nice penny". He asked me if I could make head or tail of the official description of what constitutes a hundredweight of seed potatoes. Then he read it. The legal phraseology sounded so involved and fantastic that we both roared with laughter. The conclusion we came to was that in every hundredweight of seed potatoes there must be 108 lb. of seed potatoes before it can be a hundredweight of seed potatoes. "Of course I haven't gone through it all yet," he said, taking off his spectacles, "but there will likely be a sub-section somewhere!" This business of growing food for the nation—and making a financial success of it in the by-going—has renewed his youth at seventy-five.

But the farmers of the west coast who have been stock-rearing—hill sheep, Highland and other cattle—have not been so lucky. A farmer friend of mine from one of the Islands, who had bought beasts early in the year and brought them to the October sale in the mainland mart, dropped £2 a head. I was in the ring with him at the time—as I had been some weeks earlier when he brought his lambs over. Graded lambs, of course, did well enough, but the far larger number of the others went very cheap. Even the auctioneer shook his head. "I am sorry, gentlemen, to let them go at that. But you mustn't blame me. I can't help it. If the Government will go on ploughing up ground, what can you expect?"

This was, perhaps, not so much a political hit at the Government as a reference to the excuse given by the North of England buyers that much of their pasture land had had to be ploughed up. Which did not alter the fact that the lambs were bought and bought cheap. The hill men and men of the West somehow never seem to come in for a good deal when good deals are going. The way the hill sheep-farmers in Scotland are at the moment heading for insolvency has been too well aired in the press for me to comment on it here. But to anyone who knows how large a place the lamb-sale takes in the economy of so many of our northern holdings, this year's prices made sad reading. Said one ringside wag: "Och, they'll be doing something about it—too late as usual."

All the same, farming on the whole has been doing very well, and more than one farmer has admitted to me, with a reserved light in his face: "I can't complain." A farmer must be hard put to it, as we say, before he can't complain. By the time the bank agent or "man of business" invites himself to a day at the partridges, things are snug in more places than the stackyard.

This evening, in the dusk, stacks of grain against the western sky arrested the eye. Their turreted shapes in certain lights and against certain backgrounds can have a curious appeal, an odd mixture of fantasy and solid value. Upon the autumn half-light, slowly deepening to dark, there descends occasionally a profound stillness. The air, too, was gathering its autumn chill, and in this premonition of frost the dark-brown fallen vegetation was exhaling that indescribable tang of decay, faint yet pungent, strangely pleasant, that seems half a scent and half a primeval memory. A leaf fell now here, now there, through the unmoving air. The eye followed its silent slanting descent, and not so much thought as the blood itself became conscious of fullness, of a natural process completed in all its stages and now falling out of space, through time, slowly, as in a dream. Each leaf had all the lightness of a dream-like motion, a setting out for the last time upon an individual journey.

When the day's work is over to stand in this twilight for a little is to let its cool lightness come about the mind as water in a bath about the body. Enchantment is perhaps too difficult a word to use lightly. It might be taken to imply an exotic condition of the mind, acquired by some mysterious chance. There are doubtless such conditions. But that is not what is meant here. Quite the contrary, for this simple condition of mind can be

acquired by a conscious act. It is the blessed virtue of this condition that it can be acquired by a deliberate act. And as with all
acts, the oftener it is repeated the more skilled one becomes in
achieving results. There is nothing mysterious in coming to a
standstill. To stand and not to think, receptive to the influences
of earth and sky, scent and sound and silence, is easy and
natural. But something then comes seeping in, sometimes very
slight, so slight that it scarcely seems to come at all; and yet,
if the pause be held, there supervenes a delicacy of tension, a certain strangeness within oneself and going out through the far
reaches of the world; and the burden of the day's care slowly
falls away like the leaf.

To be concerned with the solidly calculable things all the
time is surely literally, arithmetically, to become lop-sided, to
know only one aspect of living. It came to me with a small
shock the other day that I had, for example, missed the autumn
bird-life, the wheeling of great flocks of plovers over the uplands, the gatherings of excited swallows, particular grouse and
partridge coveys, the new strategic disposal of the pigeon clan.
I felt as if I had been robbed of something I could never hope to
recover! So much had been filched away by a too material pre-
occupation with affairs. Grey-brown backs went running in a
field in the deep dusk. They got up. Curlew. They affected me
with a feeling of remoteness, of experiencing a life that I had
forgotten, far back in the past—or on some other plane. The
touch of dismay seemed absurd, but it was there nevertheless,
like a warning!

The only bird I can properly say I have seen these many
weeks is the robin. That brings me back to the twilight again—
and no doubt to what some southern critics, in an apprehension
of mystery beyond our feeble reach, call the Celtic Twilight.
I have reserved for this hour the job of breaking in a piece of
fresh ground.

It is heavy work, for I am sinking the weeds deep, and therefore requires many straightenings of the back and leanings on the spade. There is no particular hurry for it. Next year seems a long time off these days. And for audience I have had a robin or two. They are fond of eating, of course. They have the name of being voracious. They are terrible fighters. But they are friendly little birds. And never in any autumn have I heard them sing as I have this autumn. And such variety too! I could swear that one of them has been practising a new kind of tune, something midway between the ringing, emphatic triumph of spring and the plaintive soliloquy of autumn. This fellow was so pleased with the two or three liquid notes at the end of his song that he kept on stringing them out to a full dozen and then a few more, combined this way and that, as if he really couldn't give up, so delighted he was. But once he deceived me.

Over by the gate there is an old elm-tree. On a twig not far from the top, on the western side, a blackbird sang through the singing season in the evening hour. It was a rich outpouring, for on occasion the blackbird can be hesitant enough and full of pauses. I observed that when the true ecstasy was upon him, he was invariably facing the west. Well, from this twig the other evening came a song like a pale memory of the blackbird's. Listening, I decided it was a young thrush, not very sure of himself, but I could not see the bird because the darkness was so deep. I threw up a pebble among the branches, and, against the sky, caught the characteristic swoop of the robin that, among his other odd habits, all too manifestly likes to sit, when I am not there, on top of my spade.

The Factor's Tale

In war days of restricted travel there is a special pleasure in coming upon one of those privately published books of memoirs which, though overwhelmingly devoted to personal and family affairs, yet now and then throw revealing flashes on "protected" places once intimately known—as intimately as I knew Gress and Stornoway in Lewis. I have just been browsing through such a book written, when he was over eighty, by Evander Maciver, who was born in Gress, near Stornoway, in 1811, and who in his time was factor to more than one Highland landlord, including the Duke of Sutherland.

Factors in the Highlands may not have had an enviable name ever since those bitter days of the clearances, but Mr. Maciver was one of nobler mould, and though there may be those of us who disagree with some of his opinions concerning the treatment of certain basic economic matters in the Highland scheme of things, yet his attitude was just and, whenever possible, generous. Perhaps, too, it has an interest of novelty to look on the Highlands through a factor's eyes. And in any case the sociological picture is never complete without him.

But if only he had thought it worth his while to describe in some detail the active life of a town like Stornoway, where his father carried on so many different kinds of business in the beginning of last century! But presumably the matter was too ordinary, too unimportant (as, in truth, surrounding workaday life generally is to most of us), though interesting facts do come through. I have sometimes wondered why in such times people went out of their way to get a friendly traveller to carry a letter or dispatch for them. There was no censorship in the Highlands in those days, and I could not believe that our postal service was unreliable. The reason is now clear. A letter from Stornoway to London cost one shilling and fivepence halfpenny, and if any "extra" was enclosed, such as a cheque or a bill, it cost double. Mr. Maciver's mail to London often ran to pounds sterling. Up until 1832 there was one sloop a week to and from Poolewe, and for it to be held up a month by bad weather was not un-usual. After 1832 the Government were prevailed upon to pay a little more, and the sloop did its best to run twice a week. Within a century we were flying the passage in a few minutes!

Evander Maciver, who died as recently as 1903, was in his last year at Edinburgh Academy when on one occasion he was called upon by the teacher to read from a chapter of Xenophon's *Anabasis* in Greek for the benefit of two gentlemen who had come into the classroom, "as visitors often did. One of them," records Maciver, "was a heavy, dull, red-faced, grey-haired gentleman, who kept his head and face down without the smallest appearance of animation. He was well known to many of my schoolfellows, and the whisper went round at once that he was Sir Walter Scott."

But his story of mutiny and shooting and the burying of

silver dollars in the sands north of Stornoway harbour is his outstanding "incident". He was a boy of fourteen at the time, and what he specially remembers "was the arrival at the Custom House of several carts loaded with silver dollars, and the turnout of the whole people of Stornoway, old and young, male and female, to see such a wonderful and rare sight as cartloads of silver in the streets of the town".

The story is a grim one with a grim ending. Some six or seven seamen, including a boy, had landed inside Chicken Head, near the farm of Swordale, and taken refuge in a cave. They said their vessel had sunk, but they had managed to escape in a small boat. When news of the shipwreck reached the Custom House two officers went along to the cave to investigate and help. Most of the crew came from the Fife coast, and there was one Frenchman, a tough, sulky fellow. They duly provided all necessary particulars relating to the lost vessel, and the officers, satisfied, were on their way back to the Custom House when they were overtaken by the panting boy. And there and then, in broken English, he stammered out his extraordinary tale. The captain of the ship and the supercargo had been murdered by the mate and the cook. There were casks of silver dollars on board. The murderers got the rest of the crew to join in with them by offering them a share of the dollars. The dollars were divided up among them. They cut up all the canvas on board and sewed it into bags. Each sailor bagged his pile, and the whole treasure was now buried in the sands of the cave.

The officers had no more than got a grip on these astonishing assertions when the mate hove in sight, spoke "angrily and roughly" to the boy, and ordered him back to the cave forthwith.

"But the Customs gentlemen took the part of the boy", brought him with them to Stornoway, and reported the matter to the authorities. The next day a party set out for the cave, with orders to apprehend the crew and take possession of their effects. The bags of dollars were duly found and carried to Swordale, "where they were deposited for the night" in the barn. The following day the farm carts bore the treasure to the Custom House through the seething populace, and "the crew were lodged in a hotel" under the eye of the magistrates, for Stornoway had no Procurator-Fiscal, and the Sheriff-substitute was away on his farm near Gairloch.

In fact, all was accomplished in such a decent and leisurely way that "a considerable amount" of the silver was deemed to have "been abstracted, but by whom or by what means never transpired", while it lay overnight in the barn. Silver dollars for a year or two entered the Stornoway currency and were regularly given as part of the change for a pound note. The following year Mr. Maciver carried away with him "several dollars, for each of which I got three shilllings and tenpence from a silversmith on the North Bridge, Edinburgh".

However, an investigation was held and lasted for several days, after which it was thought advisable to report the whole affair to the Lord Advocate. In the course of time a revenue cutter arrived from Leith and relieved Stornoway of the mariners and the dollars (excepting those retained privately), and then came a second time for a cargo of witnesses.

At the trial many things became clear. The vessel was a schooner bound for South America from Malta, and the boy had been put on board at Malta by his father just to see if he would really like to be a sailor. The father arranged that he would sleep with the captain, and so it came about that he actually saw the captain being shot, while he heard the fight and shot which disposed of the supercargo.

The cargo of olive oil and beeswax belonged to the supercargo, as did the thousands of silver dollars, which, with a private word to the captain, he had packed in strong casks and placed in the hold. But the captain in a weak if human moment (for conversational material was limited on such a voyage) told the mate of the specie. Now, the cook was on the mate's watch, and in a still weaker moment the mate (a Scot) told the cook (a Frenchman). The cook hatched the plot and persuaded the mate. Sending the rest of the crew to sleep, the Auld Alliance battened them down and set about their foul and murderous deeds. At the trial the rest turned King's evidence, and the two were found guilty "and were hanged at high-water mark at Leith".

If instead of translating Xenophon in class the young Maciver had given his personal account of this story, one wonders what effect it would have had on the heavy, dull, red-faced gentleman who kept his face down without the smallest appearance of animation.

To the West

It is a calm sunny day, and as the curving train leaves the fertile valley that leads to Strathpeffer its speed slackens and it begins to puff-puff mightily up the slope to Achterneed. There it rests for a little amid tidy flower-plots, before once more puffing on and up into the heather—and then down through the birches into Garve, with its blue-gleaming hill loch.

The burns are in flood after recent rains. Here is a river whose peat-dark water comes rushing into the neck of a pool, broadens in diminishing swirls, tails off into calm, then gathers again into a smooth-gliding outlet. What a lovely thing is a pool which the eye can encompass in a glance! And there, at the edge of the broken water, is the place where a salmon lies. You would cast the fly out over the stream and cunningly bring it round until . . . But the train goes on, and tries to persuade you that a small hill loch, with dark wind ripples, is a lovelier sight

than a river pool. Keep the boat far enough away to let the tail
fly land a yard from the weed. . . .

Climbing still, with the country growing barer, more austere,
until at last we approach the watershed and draw into Achnasheen station.

Folk get off and you look at them through the window. The
train stands in the sun. The naked sunlight is pervaded by an
immense quietude, intensified by the soft hissing of escaping
steam. The green door of the hotel needs paint, as if the sun had
eaten into it, and into the building stone, over a long period of
time. Presumably the guard has been relieved, for he walks
along the off platform carrying his lamp and his leather satchel
with the red and the green flags tucked under the flap. Time
stops altogether. A lay preacher, with a heavy country tread,
wearing dark clothes, a white collar, and dickey but no tie,
comes up the platform, glancing in at the windows in an almost
secretive way; then down the platform, his heavy tread quite
noiseless. He is probably searching for a vacant compartment, or
for someone, or for some spiritual conjunction beyond the
mind's grasp. Then no one at all moves anywhere, and the
station is like a wayside station in a desert under the burning
sun, with leagues of sand and scrub—and the soft hiss of escaping steam.

To break the spell, I get up and hang out of the window. A
country lad leans out of a neighbouring window and asks a man
who has descended from his carriage if this train goes to Kyle.

"Ay, they cross here," answers the man.

"Do I have to change here for Kyle?"

"What's that?" The man does not understand. Change here?
On a single-line track! . . . "This is the Kyle train."

"Oh, it's the Kyle train."

A long time after, the train from Kyle draws in, illustrating
more clearly than ever before, as we seem to glide past windows
with staring faces, the elusive theory of relativity.

Two men come into our carriage, and one asks the other:
"Did you see the spaniel go down on to the line just now and
under the carriage?"

"No, I didn't notice, but——"

"Isn't that dangerous? What if the train suddenly started?"

"Oh, it's all right. He's had his lesson. He once got the right
side of his jaw skinned off by the wheel of the engine. He's had
his lesson."

"But I saw him going under just now. How could he have
had his lesson?"

"Well, he's had it anyway."

"I mean it doesn't seem to have done him much good."

"Perhaps not."

Heraldic cloud-shadows lay here and there on the green hills
behind Achnasheen. The train from Kyle moved out of the
station. The lay preacher walked down the off platform. The
silence came in about us. From the heart of this timelessness our
train slowly drew out.

Down past Achnashellach, with its gardens, striking varieties
of trees, and long views into the hills, and on to Lochcarron and
the first sight of the brown seaweed on the western shore.

The western shore. The western ocean. Haunting syllables for
that ocean from old Norse and Gaelic invade the mind, and
presently—it often happens on such a journey—the mind finds
itself, in the midst of an imaginary discussion, giving sound
advice. The figure to whom this advice is given may or may not
be clearly discerned, may hardly even be known, but the mind
knows it intimately. "When folk," says the mind, "who flatter
themselves that they are practical, smile in a superior way and
suggest that you are vague and poetic because you delight in
those haunting syllables, that you are a devotee of the Celtic
twilight, don't let them off with it whatever you do; on the
contrary, smile back and say . . ." But the train swings round
and discloses a white yacht at anchor before Plockton, and in

the presence of such grace and beauty the mind relapses gratefully into silence.

Has man yet created anything more beautiful than a sailing yacht? . . . The nostrils begin to twitch. Yes, it's Kyle of Lochalsh, the terminus, thick with a smell of cured herring and noisy with shunting engines. We have reached the West. There will be trains no more.

The *Lochmor* is at one pier—but where is the *Lochness*? Ah, here she comes, high above the water, like the illustration in the advertisement, with all Skye for background. This capacity of the West for providing scenery is uncanny. Wherever one looks, there it is in its most luring shapes, with an atmosphere about it slightly incredible, like the atmosphere the mind puts about a legend.

Idly one tries to analyse this effect, for there is no hurry any more. The principal component may be the amount of light reflected from the sea into the aqueous air; or, rather, the way in which that light gets broken up by islands and headlands, so that there is no vast cold stretch of water rising to a remote horizon, no grey sameness of a sea, but, on the contrary, bays and inlets, tidal races and skerries, sea-birds and seals—the ocean, with all its impulses quickened, searching out the land. And the land plays the weirdest tricks with the light that the sea reflects, so that never does any part of that land appear twice the same.

Long after we have eaten, cargo is still being loaded. We stand watching the slings of varied goods being lowered into the forward hold. The man on the winch is extremely expert. When the lads on the pier have whacked the sling tight—with the sound an angry cattleman gets out of the hide of a beast—he heaves away carefully; then, with his load swinging over the hold, like a golfer swinging his putter, he seizes the perfect moment to slip the lot down the hole. We stand silently watching the process.

At the end of an hour we lift our heads and think, ah! now we are off, but yet another railway wagon gets pushed into position and the loading goes on. Bags of onions, barrels of paraffin, garage tools, beds, everything you couldn't readily think of, live fowls and three squealing pigs, even fish in the boxes of a well-known English combine: white fish from Aberdeen—for Stornoway!

Our eyes are drawn to a ten-ton yacht in full sail making up into Loch Duich. But even she seems to move slowly, as if life were without moorings, and we contemplate her for a long time. Probably she is going through the narrows, by Kyle Rhea and Isle Ornsay for Mallaig—or the Small Isles; perhaps to drop anchor off the white sands of Eigg. Not many corners down in that wonder world that we do not know. From the sky, she cannot have anything but a sparkling passage.

But here we are, off ourselves at last, little more than two hours late, with the sugar loaf of Raasay dark violet against a sky now being veiled by its high thin streamers of wind cloud. It's a good world. The land on either hand is sun-drowsed, the rocks smooth and rounded and ageless. Two hours late? And they have lain like that since long before our time began, lifting their smooth shoulders out of grass and heather! Mile after mile of rock and heath, uninhabited and utterly still. The immemorial heedlessness touches the mind.

But the sea moves in short waves, low and glistening and white-tipped, and overhead the gulls balance and dip, swoop and rise, with a flawless art. We head for Applecross, the dark Cuillin behind us sharply ridged against an opalescent sky with banks of clearly defined white cloud here and there on their shoulders. We pick up the small boat coming out from Applecross. Long sweeps in a long slow pull. The rope is caught. The boatmen hang on. A man and his little girl come aboard. Goods and four hikers go off. All clear!... and they drift astern on the rapid river from the ship's screw. The great event of the day in Applecross is over.

Raasay falls behind—and here is Rona, the north point, with its lighthouse. The lighthouse itself and the gable-ends of the keepers' houses are brilliantly defined against the western sky and convey the impression, startlingly distinct, of an eastern temple. The mind gets so lost that the body starts violently when a lap-dog yelps from the other side of the seat right in the ear. The high thin voices of three southern ladies exclaim in amusement, crying, "Now you mustn't!" and they fondle the fattened body with its lolling tongue. Then they cry to one another, "How marvellous!" as the gulls, without a wing-beat, keep abreast of the ship's galley. "However do they do it? Isn't it too wonderful!" There comes a moment when scraps are thrown overboard. The excitement of that moment is sometimes so much for the gulls that they lighten ship before diving. They were weaving their patterns directly overhead. I moved away, trusting if things happened thus and thus—at least to the lap-dog—it would be from out the provenance of Allah.

The headlands of the north-east of Skye, in a thin veil of mist, bring back memories of our own old boat, for it was out past Ruadh Hunish towards Fladdachuain that we had our trial run —before laying our first course one fine and exciting day on Waternish Point. Memory is already at its strange fond work on that enthralling if foolhardy adventure, and the gardener herself at an odd time wonders if it really did take place, for it can have for her a certain dream-like quality, as of something that happened "somewhere else".

The small round knob of Fladdachuain fades out and we come abreast of the Shiant Isles, with the hills of Harris to the south'ard, and the grey-blue land of Lewis behind and stretching out of sight far to the north. I grow aware of voices behind me for the first time, and vaguely glimpse a manly shoulder in ship's uniform and another in black broadcloth.

"Do you know what he said then?"

"No," answered the blue uniform.

"He said," replied the clerical broadcloth, "he said: 'And then for the first time I entered into the clear bright sunlight of pure agnosticism'!"

"'Of pure agnosticism'!"

They both laughed, marvelling in rich satire at the joke.

"Oh but," said the ship's blue, "Maclean would give him his answer to that."

"He did. He did that. But—'the clear bright sunlight of pure agnosticism'!"

They doubled over, then stretched their legs against the next sally.

I began to pick up the deep sea-lochs in Lewis, and to wonder where adventure would actually take us. There were certain yachting promises, but war now seemed very near, and this might be the last trip to the West for a long time, perhaps the very last. Beyond all I wished to find out a few things, some no more tangible than attitudes of mind in old and young, as though I would put my early memories to an objective test before it was too late. Perhaps it went deeper, down among the roots of an old way of life that might vanish entirely....

The Eye peninsula—with Stornoway a smother of smoke on its near side. Then the lighthouse and Stornoway bay. Here is Maciver's coaling hulk—that great old hull of a windjammer, with her yacht-like bows and fine rake aft. She is worth a visit, were it only to stare at her capstans and imagine the tread of the circling feet and the throaty notes of a sea shanty. We go along the line of Norwegian and Swedish vessels at their moorings, with deck cargoes of barrels. The steam drifters (Stornoway is in the middle of its herring season) sell their catches of mackerel at two shillings a basket to these hardy Scandinavians who cure them on the spot, until, with a full cargo worth a large sum of money, they return home.

TO THE WEST

Now the steamer has arrived and here we are, as eager to be off as the next. A wave to a friendly face in the crowd on the pier—for this is Stornoway's moment—and we clatter down the gangway, and along a winding avenue through the concourse, to the waiting cars. "So you've come!" They are a kind, hospitable folk in Stornoway.

In Lewis

That first morning stroll to the pier and the meeting with two or three fish-curers, old friends, is as pleasant as the light that sparkles on the waters past Goat Island and out to the Point.

"How's the fishing?"

"Bad. Very bad."

The drifters are lying alongside, nets neatly piled, and no stir of life. Every night they go out, and every morning come back with the same story. "You wonder sometimes how they can have the heart to do it. Expenses piling up. Calm and cheerful. They are triers, and no mistake."

We walk up and down and I get all the news. This absence of a fishing has a certain gloom. These curers do not complain of their own lack of business. Their sympathies are with the seamen, who work hard to catch nothing (except debt), and who can weather the financial loss less easily. In the evening—

for the most likely grounds, as it happens, are not far away—to watch them, boat after boat, setting out, is to have the emotion of sympathy touch the heart. For I hardly know of a more gallant sight than a drifter heading out of a spacious harbour at full speed for the open sea, all shipshape, nets ready, men standing about the deck, with a rush of foam at the forefoot. The gamble of the deep. Night after night after night they have drawn a blank. But perhaps this night? Not so long ago one of these boats shot her nets somewhere off Skye, hauled over sixty crans, made for Mallaig, and realized in cash just over £250. Such a stroke of luck does not come too often. But it can come.

So the gloom is irradiated with hope, as the sea with light. And what work they can pack into twenty-four hours when the herring do come on the ground! No ca'-canny, no eight-hour day then. The main problem is to defeat sleep. It is an adventure for ever creating new stories, and in the saloon bar of the Caley we hear a few, from the Highlands, from Donegal, from Lowestoft, or Norway, or Grimsby.

Here is one from Ireland, told that morning by a quiet-mannered curer with a Scots tongue, a dry humour, and a belief that he is practically teetotal.

Anyway, he was very illuminating about conditions on a certain part of the west of Ireland while he was opening up curing there many years ago. "I got on well with the Irish," he said. "They are all right, if you know how to take them. I always took them that same way. If it's a new bit of ground you're wanting for a curing station, the crofter will ask enough to buy half Ireland. He thinks you're made of money. But after a while, the priest comes in and it's settled at once. No trouble. Sensible fellows, these priests, free and easy. Oh, I got on fine with them. One day when I was over at B—— a fellow I'd done a good turn for asked me if I ever put anything on a horse. 'No,' I replied truthfully, 'I never bet.' 'Sure, that's the great pity,' he said, 'for I have a dead snip.' Well, he named the horse in a whisper, and it must have stuck in my mind, for when I went back I told a friend of mine, a local chap, and within half an hour that whole village had it, and to a man they put their shirts on it. The horse came in first."

"And you didn't put anything on yourself?"

"Ay, I made thirty-four pounds. But if you'd seen that village! For over two whole days not a stroke of work was done by anybody. All the champagne from near and far was drunk off first, and then they settled down to it. After breakfast the following morning they were still there. When I came out from my lunch, some were gone, but there were a few new faces, and only one or two old ones. By the following forenoon, I think I was the only old face left among the lot. I was stopping at the inn, you understand, and thirty-odd pounds could go a long way then. So I thought it might be as well to get a breath of fresh air. There was an open sort of charabanc belonging to the place, and we got the fellow who could drive it, and he managed to start it after a while, and we set off. We had a nice ride, and the charabanc stopped at a few places. Then we came to a wayside inn and found it shut. Perhaps it was getting a bit late by this time, though I don't think so, because it was now daylight again. Anyway, a window over the door went up and a man's face hung out, looking down on us. I nodded to him, for I remembered he had stuck it until yesterday afternoon, and he was a hearty fellow, who would take drink for drink with you and would see that you took it, too. But he wasn't in a good way at that moment. As he gaped at me, you could see his grey face open in astonishment. Then he gasped: 'B'jasus, is it still you?'"

Not that there is much drinking done in Stornoway, or no more than in any other town of the size. There are whole drifter crews that do not touch liquor, but if you go out for a night with one of them and take a bottle with you for luck and good fellowship, the skipper may disarm your surprise in the pleasantest way by accepting the gift for the medicine-chest. The sea breeds a great tolerance.

Many of the crews, too, are quietly religious men. Yet these extraordinary religious revivals that were now taking place in Lewis are for the most part confined to the purely crofting townships. Revivals among fishing communities, from Lerwick to Cornwall, have not been uncommon in the past, and explanation has been sought amongst the emotions that the sea, with life and death in its arms, can so readily and vividly evoke. Crofters are for the most part more immune from spiritual upheaval, being rooted in the earth with its slow-moving seasons.

Out here, however, sea and land come close together and as news reached us of one place after another "going down" with "the revival", I could not help wondering. Much sensible talk there was of adverse economic conditions and especially of the demoralizing effects of "the dole" on a community for which it was never designed. But I was not quite satisfied with the most searching explanations, even when they became knowledgeably psychoanalytic. I knew the high unemployment rate on the Island. I had myself investigated and advised upon claims for the dole. On the practical or economic side I had not a great deal to learn, and I could make fairly precise comparisons with other places in Scotland where unemployment also ran high. After nights of talk, I merely knew that here was something I did not really understand.

I do not profess to understand it yet, for that first effort of mine to attend a religious revival meeting seems in retrospect even more strange than what we set out to discover. That I may not here name the little township or people concerned is of no importance. That it is difficult to convey weird psychic effects, that seemed at once so illusive, and yet so momentarily real, is obvious. Again, these meetings for the most part took place in private houses, and, naturally, one cannot intrude into a private house out of a spirit of mere curiosity. Some newspaper correspondents had done this, and those concerned were naturally angry about the reports that appeared in the public press, whereby what was to them a matter of profound religious emotion was made matter for cheap sensationalism. I sympathized deeply with this attitude. Any manifestation of spiritual life, in whatever form it may take, even the extreme form of apparent hysteria, may have come to be regarded too readily by us with scepticism, if not with discomfort and some contempt.

These meetings do not begin until late in the evening and frequently go on until four or five in the morning. As we drove through the township at midsummer midnight a single light was on in each house, but in one house all four windows were lit up. "That's the place," whispered my friend, who had the wheel.

We found ourselves talking in low voices, and when we reached the home of the local man who was to conduct us to the meeting, we were in a properly receptive mood. Our intelligent host had been anticipating our arrival with a certain misgiving, and I at once tried to put him at his ease by saying that I realized the delicacy of the situation and would, after all, rather not go. This induced the state of indecision which can last for hours and is in so many ways typical of the West. It is often a very wonderful state, full of subtle undercurrents of thought and intuition. You do everything except reach a definite conclusion. But in process of time the pattern of decision forms itself. We travelled from the East, from Buddha and Pantanjali; we touched upon the shamanistic studies of anthropologists and the mysticism of the medieval church; we sat amid the visions of St. Columba on a Hebridean island.

"You have no idea," said our host, his eyes shining in the soft paraffin light, "of how the very atmosphere is charged with this religious feeling. You cannot get away from it. It is palpable. It hits you. It is nothing—and yet it is everything. You could never believe it—until you lived amongst it. They go into

trances. They cry out. They moan. They stretch their hands.
But it's not merely that; it's—I don't know what. It's easy to
be critical, to analyse, but—there is a core, a something, and it's
that *something* that is the mysterious force, that *something*—
whatever it is!" and he spread his fingers with a Gallic gesture.

Presumably I had shown some understanding and made it
clear that I would never dream of going to the meeting, for he
suddenly decided that it was time we set out. It was now two
o'clock in the morning. We went out into a dark-grey world to
find the close-packed rain descending in vertical lines. We
approached the township, where all the lights were as before.
But the meeting was just over and folk were standing about in
the rain, which they heeded not.

Our host was disappointed. The meeting should now have
been at the height of its power. We discreetly drove past the
house and drew up. In a startling way, two figures materialized
by our side windows. A voice said we had fulfilled a prophecy,
for though it was known we were coming, yet hope had been
given up by all except by the voice—which belonged to a
young man who now entered and took the fourth seat in our
car. His words of greeting were, "The arm of the Lord was
made manifest to-night in a wonderful manner. Not often have
we so powerfully felt among us the presence of our Redeemer,
Jesus Christ . . ." A young voice, with an urge in it to be pleasant and happy. I was disappointed that it was not a Lewis voice,
not even a Highland voice. But "Quite!" said our host, with
his perfect manners. The voice went on. At the first moment
our host interposed again, agreeably. A third and a fourth time,
at lengthening intervals, he nodded: "Quite so."

But the stream of the young man's oratory was too constant,
too strong, and I have a memory of our three heads bowed at
last, silent, like boulders in a river, throughout a long period of
time. Actually it was not much more than an hour—about an
hour and ten minutes as far as we could calculate afterwards.

But it seemed a new kind of time, and I once awoke from a reverie, induced by a quotation from Micah, that was like a waking from sleep. I looked at the other two heads, bowed still. And the river flowed on under the drumming rain, with the queer grey light outside, a lamp in a window, and a solitary figure passing like a wraith.

At last I did my best to move, perhaps in some vague effort to emulate my host's politeness, perhaps in some dim but still genuine curiosity, and asked this religious young leader what happened exactly in the mind of the person who all at once became greatly conscious of "the spirit of God moving in him". In particular, I have a feeling that we all wanted "to *see* the light". But I fear that we were still involuntary thralls to the merely analytical, for the car remained dark. Everything was put down quite naturally to the presence of God, to the spirit of Christ Jesus, who redeems us from our sins. In a subsequent effort at discussion we found ourselves considering the state of the world, wars and rumours of wars, and, of course, politics. Yes, he had been a Trade Unionist, a Socialist. Did he still believe in Socialism? "When you have seen the greed and the graft and the jealousies and the strife"—I will not try even to indicate his amazing resource in biblical quotation—"you despair of the materialistic doctrines of any worldly creed. I am no longer for or against any political party. The Lord welcomes everyone, whatever his political or economic beliefs. All I am sure of is that the present state of the world is a result of godlessness, a falling away from God's grace, and that no material beliefs can ever put it right. As St. Paul said, writing to . . ." And he was off once more.

It remained a youthful voice, anxious to have gladness in it, and having gladness in it; a young man prepared for personal rebuffs, who had received personal rebuffs, but was hanging on to some revelation inside him that induced a state of humility. How deeply in his nature this humility was founded might be a matter for thought, were it not that to look for the perfect humility would be foolish, even had we still been capable of looking. There was, above and over all, the note of serenity, that tone of gladness, like something memoried or legendary. It might be destroyed as swiftly as it had come; it might be the efflux either of a sanguine or of a potentially hysteric nature; it may have been induced by a life of continuous economic uncertainty and hardship, for he knew many kinds of occupations, some of them invariably accompanied by small but harrowing personal humiliations (a Paisley woman had notably rebuffed him for trying to sell her a vacuum cleaner), just as he knew unemployment and the dole; from all that, he had escaped—to find himself of some importance in the high communion of "the spiritual life"; a leader in his small way; a man listened to and followed. Here was compensation and to spare, and here the acceptance of rebuff or humiliation might be as unction to the soul.

Such analysis was easy, yet it did not satisfy, not altogether. It did not help with the "*something*—whatever it is", which remains, when all is said, at the basis of this revivalism, however characterized it may be occasionally by wild physical manifestation and an undeniable hysteria. The subject is hardly so easy as the cynic or materialist may pretend. Indeed, the attitude of the cynic or wholesale sceptic may here be highly suspect. For the cynic is too often a man who has already taken care to "escape" from responsibility before opening his mouth.

At last he shook hands with us and, after putting his head inside again for a final few words, he hoped, a smile in his voice that was propitiatory but not ingratiating, that we would come to his next meeting and enter with him into the fellowship of Christ.

"When did you say you were going away?" our host asked him, polite to the last.

"I was going on Monday—but it may be revealed to me not to go."

241

Our host understood.

The lights were gone at last; and the gable-ends of the cottages, down from the road, were like grey striding men. All at once I felt the force of the atmosphere that our host had spoken of, and realized what he had meant when he said, "It is palpable. It hits you." Here was illusion all right! For the whole place seemed to have gone psychic; the pale faces, the stationary-striding gable-ends of the cottages, the curve of the earth, the green corn, the ditches, the motionless cattle; the sensation of invisible movement unaffected by the steady windless rain; the incredible living stillness, emanating from sleep, from houses whose lights had withdrawn before the grey morning. The mind suddenly thought, *This is the place*. And the place was stranger than any place of desert and sphinx, or valley of ruined temples, or palaces of Kubla Khan, for it was ancient but it was alive, and its history was happening in it while its bodies slept. We pushed through this atmosphere and came to our host's house where we were adequately refreshed. It was now after four in the morning and high time that we set off for sea to haul nets that had been set. But we delayed. The rain came down incessantly. The sea was grey and wet. We would go home and leave the nets to a later hour. And home we went, after a final lengthy leave-taking, including a long, involved, agreeable discussion in the rain, but not before stopping once on the road to get out, and listen to an invisible sea-bird calling from the surf along the western shore, and light a cigarette, in that weird hour of mist and morning, under a sky whose sluices were open. For it is the hour when the thought of bed departs and one wonders —whither now? It is a long way home. But home like slaves we must go and to bed, for all that Pantanjali or St. Columba may be walking over the mist-veiled moors. It is the moment, none the less, when one may adventure in the clear thought that is like vision and that is emptied of fear.

Great Bernera

Southern townspeople have put it to me that Highland life must be very dull. All I can honestly say is that after ten days in Stornoway I had a wistful desire for a fortnight's peace in Edinburgh or Paris. To go to bed at five in the morning may seem a waste of time at the moment; but after many mornings one is not so sure about it. So I decided it was time that I fulfilled at least part of my original intentions and set out for Bernera—and from Bernera to the great rock-faces of the Flannan Isles in the Atlantic.

The trip across Lewis from Stornoway to Loch Roag always comes upon me with an air of surprise. In the evening light, the earth is extended into a dimension of flatness to which there seems no end. A dip of the road, a parting of the horizon haze, the gleam of a low sun, and the remoteness goes or comes. The light is a volatile essence of silver warmed with gold. And now and again it touches the mind with an intimacy very strong, as of something forgotten and found again.

So we glance at the shallow valley through which the car is

moving at an even speed, and are surprised to find that a remnant of the old shieling life still survives. Smoke is arising from a turf bothie; a young woman is standing still, looking at the car, her cattle behind her; an old bent man is also regarding us, and two young lads. Far back beyond the beginnings of recorded history, the folk drove their cattle to the summer shielings for the hill pasture and the making of butter and cheese. In that evening glow, it required little effort to realize what a pastoral life meant long ago. The folk still sing their songs, traditional songs of a haunting loveliness, about life and love at the shielings.

It is easy to grow sentimental about that ancient way of life, but foolish to do so, because life lived spontaneously is rarely sentimental. The traditional songs are never sentimental; they simply provide the evidence that many a broken heart and vivid singing mouth moved through such valleys in the ages; many a face looked at the remote horizons, many a head bowed before a beauty that quickened sorrow or gladness, despair or love, too much.

The hills of Harris, to the south, rise from the plain in a way that at first glance seems almost theatrical. One may be forgiven, in certain aspects of light and mist, for not quite believing that the scene could be so well arranged. The clouds, with striking "effects", nearly always take a hand in the work. As the eyes are held, however, the hills stand back like a mountain range guarding an unexplored land.

And so onward until at last we come to the ferry and look across at the island of Great Bernera. Our Stornoway host leaves the wheel and takes an oar with the ferryman; they talk in Gaelic, eyes glimmering in a dry friendly humour. To step down from a natural scene of great beauty to the commonplaces of human contacts may seem a swift transition, but here it is not so, because the mind is quiet and humoured, suffused with the mood of land and sea, and therefore naturally unhurried. Why should one hurry? To become fussy or anxious would be more than comical in this air. And these reserved bright eyes are ready for the unusual.

I came across an extraordinary interpretation of this attitude to haste on the night before I left Bernera, and I still do not understand it fully. We discussed it afterwards, and even our Stornoway host, who has common sense, learning, and a subtle mind, and who knows the people as his own, was also not too clear about it. It was an "item" in a concert programme. To the bare platform in the village hall, innocent of any properties, entered a young man, masked by motoring goggles. Presumably he found himself in a railway station of many platforms. For he looked at invisible signs and muttered aloud and rapidly: "Platform one to two, one to two to two . . ." and laughed. Then it was platform two to three, to three, two to three . . . and he laughed a different laugh, convulsing his body in a new way. He was like a sprite out of a wood, or a satiric demon from the underworld. Platform after platform, swiftly, with a new laugh for each, until platform seven was reached, and, in a final convulsion of mockery, he rushed off the stage. The whole performance seemed to take a very short time; or at least one experienced a mounting surprise, an increasing sense of the incredible, waiting for some final explicit meaning that never came.

Bernera is a quiet island, full of little valleys and lochs. As we drove along, cooped up like fowls inside a small van, I began to wonder what the "old man" I was going to see would be like. Those inverted commas came from the pen involuntarily, probably because I thought of him not so much as a man old in years—he would not be seventy-eight until his next birthday—as one of the generation of old men whom I had known as a boy. I had never met him, and on learning recently that he had sailed with my father long before I was born, a secret urge had come upon me to find out if what I had written about men of his early prime bore some resemblance to reality.

For I could still see them clearly through a boy's vision. Men with beards, with steady eyes and quiet manners, and an air of competence and strength. In danger at sea, they never got flurried. They would hang on the edge of disaster without relaxing a muscle. At certain festival seasons, they enjoyed themselves in mutual visiting and drinking and singing. But over all, there was that clear memory of self-reliance, of the grown man standing responsibly on his own feet, with power in his hands.

It is easy to overdraw a picture, but there is the equal danger of underdrawing it. For some mysterious reason we remain suspicious of a "good" picture but are at once convinced of a "bad" one as "the real thing". For the writer who would try to isolate the positive from the negative, the lasting from the ephemeral, the way is not easy.

There was also the more particular attitude of these grown men to a little boy, the understanding that showed itself in a word or two of greeting, a touch of the hand, but especially in a kindness of the voice and eyes. The intuition of a small boy is perhaps rarely deceived in these matters.

We got out of the grocer's van, and as he came towards me, with his grey beard and weathered face and bright blue eyes, the years were calmly wiped away. There was suddenly no difficulty, no problem at all. He smiled with the unassuming friendliness that knows no age and his quiet seaman's voice greeted me as if we were meeting after many years.

The following day we walked over the island of Bernera together and I watched him skip over a few stepping-stones with the easy balance of a young man. We climbed to a cairn that crowned the highest hill or knoll, and, with his arm-long telescope, spied out all that could be seen. His knowledge of the island and its surrounding seas was minute, and extended, with that aptitude the Gael often has for intricate genealogy, to the family life of those crofter-fishermen who have always dwelt here. It is primarily a practical knowledge, so far removed from the vague mystical dreamy conception of the Gael as to be its antithesis. Everything must be precise, a matter of fact, and the interest in human relations is unending. They listen; they question; then as enlightenment is complete, they nod: "I have you now," meaning "I understand completely." And with understanding comes the friendly smile.

Bernera is a treeless island of heather and smooth rock and lochs. In the numberless little hollows or valleys the ground is cultivated in narrow strips or lazy-beds. You come on them everywhere, and when I saw them they were heavy with two crops only: oats and potatoes. I was told that this dual rotation never alters. Because of the nature of the manure, which includes sea-weed, the ground apparently does not grow tired or exhausted. I can certainly vouch for the fact that the crops were in excellent heart. This was the more interesting because here and there beds had gone out of cultivation and the heather was already invading them.

There is something intimate and personal about these narrow strips of ground, crowding together on a slope or in a valley bottom, with a snake-twist to them often, and frequently no more than a few paces in length. This way of cultivating the peaty ground has been shown by experience to be the best. The raised beds, with ditches between, permit of a perfect drainage. For the most part they are worked by spade.

As we sat there on that hill-top, with the sun shining intermittently and a soft wind blowing, trying now and then to catch the dim outline of the Flannans far on the western horizon, I asked him about the economy of the island when he was a boy long before—nearly half a century before—the days of Old Age Pensions, not to mention the dole or other forms of recent State aid. They lived, he said, quite well, and he himself had never been ill in his life—except once, not so long ago, when he was persuaded to lie in bed for a whole day, because a doctor believed he had influenza. After enduring that day with difficulty he got out of bed, and immediately felt all right.

Serious illness had been practically unknown among them. The existing scourge of Lewis, tuberculosis, was in his child-hood unknown in fact or in traditional record. He knew the first case of this disease, who brought it to his own island, how it spread after that "by blood", and indeed can trace the whole history of the scourge, not merely in his island but in lands beyond the seas to which some of the infected went.

What emerges clearly is that the decline in physique in the people of Lewis, as of other Hebridean islands and of parts of the Western Highlands, has taken place within recent times, and, for the greater part, certainly within the lifetime of my friend.

There have been various contributing factors, but the principal one, I gathered, is the change in diet. In his young days every household had its supply of oats, barley, potatoes, salt herrings, dairy produce (for the greater part of the year), and a fairly continuous supply of fresh fish. Vegetables were eaten more, and there was a better knowledge of food values. Flour and loaf bread and tea were practically unknown. The liver of cod or ling mixed with oatmeal was part of a child's daily diet. "Our mothers used to make the liver oil pure as crystal and we would drink it and think nothing of it." In other words, they had all the vitamins.

To-day there are no boats fishing out of Bernera (where in the old days there were dozens). So there is no constant supply of fresh fish, no liver oils. The people no longer grind their oats for domestic use. Where a child in former times in these west-ern islands had an in-between snack of cream sprinkled with oatmeal, or of milk with oatcake or barley bread, now he has a cup of tea and a girdle scone baked from white flour. Tea and a flour scone at the slightest excuse, or without any excuse at all!

Next, there was the matter of school attendance. In these remote islands children had—and still have at the time of writing, though there are rumours of transport in the future— to walk to school a distance averaging one to two miles. The township roads are frequently water-logged tracks and in wet weather they reach school in damp or sodden clothes and, of course, with wet feet. A single peat fire in a classroom is hardly sufficient for drying them, even when the children are placed in a row before the fire and turned slowly as they steam.

There is still another difficulty not so readily seen or understood because it is psychological. Whereas on the mainland we have received what is called modern civilization in homeopathic doses, in these distant parts it has been unloaded upon them in bulk. From the comparative seclusion of his own home, with its familiar Gaelic ways and sounds, the child sets out for a school where he is herded with others, made to talk in an unknown tongue, and to acquire through this tongue the usual school list of subjects. The strain set up here may be judged from the fact that it is fairly common among young children not to be able to take any breakfast.

Moreover, when he reached the age of fourteen in the old days, a boy was ready to take his part in the island's economy. At seventeen he was old enough to become a hand on a fishing boat. Thus from before the period of adolescence he was already part of the social life about him; in the difficult years between fifteen and twenty he was occupied in natural and not uncongenial tasks. Over fifty years ago, schooling was a fitful matter.

But now, in the absence of sea fishing, the decline in local agriculture, and the introduction of "modern methods" to old handiwork, the young of both sexes, with little or no work to do, wait on through their 'teens until, round about twenty, they feel old enough to go south. This waiting time has undoubtedly an adverse effect on mind and body. Finally, with our modern ways of education have come our modern legislation and State aid.

As we went westward, along past the house of William Black's *Princess of Thule*, talking of the herring fishings in Wick and Fraserburgh, Stornoway and Castlebay, of the hardy resilient lads who would think nothing of walking across a whole county from sea to sea, of the "times" they had had one way or another in these distant days of his youth, the hours passed pleasantly. For one is comforted by the feeling of a routh of life, a warmth of natural living. That is not to cast an ideal glow over the past. They had their trials and glooms and tragedies, bread-winners died, children had to be fed, storm and devastation and absolute want visited them; but they had their compensations and, above all, felt that they were living in the heyday of their time. This feeling of mastering their own economy, directing their own circumstances, their own fate, has in large measure slipped from them. The too violent break with the past has bred an unhealthy doubt at to the validity of their Gaelic tradition itself.

In between all this talk we had been arranging for my friend's annual trip to the Flannan Isles, those lonely green-clad rocks we had tried to pick up on the horizon of the Atlantic. Each summer season, he takes out a boatload of over thirty sheep about a year old and carries back a load of the sheep he left there twelve months before. Two trips are necessary to evacuate all the sheep, for on the rich grazing of the Flannans they grow wonderfully, and, incidentally, produce a mutton that cannot be equalled for flavour. It seemed an arduous method of sheep-farming conducted on so small a scale, but just how arduous and adventurous I had no idea until the trip was over.

Everything, I was told, depends on the weather, and the start may have to be postponed from day to day, even week to week, for this can be one of the most dangerous seas in the world. But omens were good, and we parted for the night after the fiery-cross had been sent round the crew. The start was to be at six in the morning, and I need not stir until I got a shout. I was awake at six, and lay hearkening for a sound, until I remembered that folk on this decent island kept the Creator's time. But when by half-past seven there was still no human movement, I decided that the trip was off. Half an hour later a cup of tea was brought to me. Yes, they were going, said the lady of the gentle smile, but there was no special hurry.

Ah well, it's the West! I decided, hurrying all the same, because I did not want to keep anyone back. On the way to the boat, I met the old man and asked, "Were you waiting for me?"

"No," he answered pleasantly. "We are just waiting for Alastair's cow to calf."

Now, the previous day, from early morning till late at night, Alastair and I had become friends in the way that it takes a recalcitrant Kelvin engine to make men friends. Hour after hour we had worked at it, analysed each piece of machinery, and said all that could be said—and often a little more. For Alastair was first engineer and I was signing on as his next in command. I flattered myself, after my experience with my own boat's engine, that there was nothing about a Kelvin I didn't know inside out. But I was wrong. There was a piece of mechanism called an "impulse starter" which I had never met. About nine o'clock at night we decided that a certain two springs were weak, and I got into a telephone box to ring up a man in Stornoway who had those springs. I made first contact in Carloway, and after that a voice answered me from here and there over the island, from any place but Stornoway. Supposing someone was ill, I asked, how could contact be made with a doctor, how could arrangements be made for an urgent hospital case to Stornoway? Just couldn't be done! was the answer. It seemed a bit madder than usual even for the West. Bernera alone carries a population of some five or six hundred. But there it was. We had already asked an engineer in Stornoway to stand by for a call about nine o'clock. We had made arrangements for any necessary piece of mechanism to be brought over in a private car. And here we were, unable to get in touch! We went back to the engine and fixed her up sufficiently well to do the passage—with any luck.

During these arduous proceedings I had not heard about the cow, but it now seemed she was a fortnight overdue, and as there had been trouble at the last birth—well, she was a good cow and we all appreciated Alastair's feelings. Two new members of the crew were on the scene, young limber fellows, and the third—to make six of us in all—was due to be picked up *en route*. Everything was got shipshape. Then we all went and had a solemn look at the cow. Alastair thought she might calf in an hour. We hung about for over an hour, then decided to go home. It was a good sea day. It looked as if we could not now get to the Flannans before dark, and I wanted photographs of certain rock-faces. But clearly the chances were we would not now go this day. Perhaps to-morrow . . .

It was a pity, but no one was upset. In ships' charter-parties there is always allowance made for what is called an Act of God. As for the ordinary mortal who could not have foreseen its application to the behaviour of a cow, he is always learning. The Skipper and I presently parted, with the suggestion on his side that I should complete my sleep. About eleven o'clock I was brought a bowl of thick cream and a saucer of raw oatmeal. I sprinkled the oatmeal over the cream and, as I supped, remembered my distant childhood, for not since then had I seen this rich concoction. I decided to go outside and have a last look towards the sea. A figure, coming, saw me, paused, and began to semaphore.

That wise brute of a cow had at last given birth to a calf as black as herself and bigger than any brand-new calf I had ever seen. Alastair was smiling and gave the starting-handle of the old engine so firm a swing that it hit back at him, knocking his wrist useless for the time being and turning his colour grey. He had, besides, been up all night with the cow. One of the young men got on to the handle, and after half an hour we had the engine warm enough to keep going. Once hot, we knew she would be all right. Soon the anchor was up and we were heading out of the inlet, barely six hours late. I looked at Alastair, saw he was grey still, and remembered the bottle of medicine I had brought for just such an emergency as this.

Folk may talk as they like about our Caledonian spirit, and there is, no doubt, a time for all things. Scientifically, however, one is compelled to recognize the evidence of the senses, and if what happened to Alastair in a few moments was not the result of my medicine, then it was a pure miracle.

We had a long, long wait for a man at a pier over in Lewis; but the third Kenneth did not keep us waiting and leapt nimbly from his native rock. Our crew was now complete, and we set off for an island where grazed the young sheep that were to be taken to the Flannans. I began wondering how, without any dogs, they would gather the sheep and get them on board. My wonder increased when the boat slowed up opposite a spit of rock, for there was obviously no pier, no suggestion even of a primitive jetty. The four members of the crew leapt ashore, leaving the old man (our Skipper) and myself to make fast the boat by the rock. I watched them disappear over the low crest of the island. There was silence for a long time, then a distant shouting, then sheep coming round above the west shore—followed by four men spread out, waving their arms, and whooping. I could not help laughing. It was like the boyhood game of Red Indians. When the sheep saw us and the boat, they stopped. This was the first difficult moment. The whooping increased. The sheep came on a little; then stopped again. One sheep turned its head away, seeking escape. Before the thought had got right into that solitary head, however, one of the lads had torn a soft turf from the ground and let fly. There was a burst of moss on the forehead and—the sheep came on. Came on and paused again. Swung to this side, to that. But came on; inexorably driven by the whooping, by the flailing arms and jumping feet of the nimble shepherds. Surely they would never come on to the rock, to the bare rock? They were now against it, crowding together. While we on board kept quiet and motionless, the whooping behind closed its ranks, cunning in sheep knowledge, grew ever more urgent, compulsive, until something must break. One sheep came on to the rock; two, three . . . Over the rock towards the boat, crowding, pushing, until the weight behind made one sheep jump on deck; two, three . . . The Skipper caught the first one and dropped it down into the hold, then the second, the third . . . In a few minutes we were pushing off from the rock, two of us with our heads hanging down into the hold and agreeing that the full load consisted of either thirty or thirty-one.

It had been quite an exhilarating bit of work, attended by luck, too, for if the sheep had at any moment broken back through the cordon, it would have been much more difficult to drive them a second time. Keep them on the run; don't let them think; and, above all, don't let them know they can break through.

It was now after two o'clock, and though I did not feel hungry—for a bowl of thick cream mixed with raw oatmeal is hardly an evanescent delicacy—I accepted a lump of new white bread, a solid hunk of cheese, and a dish of undeniable tea. For it was farewell to Bernera at last, and now for the Flannan Isles.

To the Flannan Isles

Seasickness is a curious sort of curse. For those who are liable to it, the sea is a place of dread, if not of horror. There are people who maintain that you expect to get seasick, therefore you will. I am quite sure that is mostly wrong. Yet the mind must have a considerable amount to do with it. Two years before, when my wife and I started off alone in our small cruiser, both of us expected to be seasick. But we did not worry about it, because, even seasick, one can manage a reasonably sized boat. We were at sea for over two months and during that time slept ashore only three nights. We experienced some very bad weather, and not least when swinging and tossing at anchor in some windy bay. Yet during all that time neither of us had a suggestion of seasickness. The theory we came to was that responsibility for keeping the boat afloat did not give us time to be seasick! The stormiest sea we found exciting and, at moments, exhilarating.

The many miles of ocean between Bernera and the Flannans

are not often calm, and as we stood out, close by Gallan Head, we could see it was not exactly smooth to-day. The heavy cross-swell was boiling on the skerries, smashing against the rock walls, and spouting upward from blue, through living green, to purest white. How wildly Gallan Head boils its cauldron! One of the crew, a young man who has sailed to South America, said this was a more dangerous piece of sea than is likely to be met most places. Apparently the tide runs for twelve hours in each direction, so that a counter-wind has time to pile up the waters in an exceptional manner. For the rest, there was nothing between us and America, barring St. Kilda. The *Rhoda* is thirty-five feet long and, with her stern cut away in Zulu fashion, is a splendid sea-boat. She rose and slid down and rolled with that complicated living action which, if one had to move at all, made one move warily. I anchored myself in a corner on deck, and lying back, admired the rock walls of that wild western coast. To the south, Scarpa Island could be discerned, a great haunt of sea-birds. The sun pierced the heavy cloud here and there with fiery beams of light. "We'll have a good passage," said the Skipper quietly.

After an hour or two I began to feel the chill of the sea, and getting up was, in a moment and to my complete surprise, properly sick. I wonder if it will ever be possible for a man to surmount the feeling of humiliation, touched with anger, at being seasick? I doubt it. But when Kenneth heard of the cream and the raw meal and the cheese, he nodded sympathetically. "Do you know," he said, "that if I take that cream and meal I feel it heavy on me for two days. In fact, I would have been sick myself." Which is, at least, an illustration of the courtesy that can be encountered in these parts!

An hour or so later, I went below, where the fire was warm and an oily smell of cooking fish arose with the steam from the open pot.

This triangle in the bow of the boat, with its bunks on either side, is what east-coast fishermen call "the den". Its atmosphere is necessarily somewhat tangible at the best of times. When things have to be battened down, it can be very rich. It was nice and thick now, and when the Skipper lit up his pipe with its load of black twist, I tried a cigarette myself. I was still not feeling on top of the weather, and it was decided that perhaps a little of the medicine that had succeeded so well with Alastair might do no harm. So we toasted each other in friendly tones. I was reclining on a bare wooden seat, but did not feel it hard, and the hand at the wheel was sympathetic enough to the seas to keep me from being violently thrown off. What an art the business of steering is! Any member of the crew in his bunk (as one of them remarked later) could tell at once when the Skipper himself took the wheel, for he alone knew all the movements of the sea and met them with the smooth certainty of the master. In real danger, they would not let him leave the wheel.

As we chatted away in the yellow light of the oil-lamp, I asked him if he had ever encountered really dirty weather on this trip. He smiled. Many a time that! And the worst was not so many years ago. On that occasion, a storm beat up while they were in the shelter of the Flannan rocks, and they lay there for days. Solid walls of sea came in through the narrow canyon between the two islands. "The boat all over was a lather of foam bubbles." Then the wind began to shift, and their position became extremely perilous. In fact, the only thing for it was to take to sea and risk it. And this they did. A steam drifter, caught in that storm, could not believe her eyes when she came on them making for land, and with the gallantry of the sea, of which ordinarily we hear so little, stood by them hour after hour. "It was a stormy passage. At home they thought we were lost, for they had no word of us all these days. But she's a good boat."

Later, one of the crew told me the real story. The Skipper, of course, was permanently fixed at the wheel, with their lives in his steering hand, looking ahead and looking behind. From behind every now and then came a vast sea. You saw it coming far off like a mountain, and if you could, you got out of its way by steering to either hand. Every sea had to be watched and dealt with, hour after hour, while the spindrift blew from the racing crests, and water, little by little, was shipped. "I never thought we'd live through it. I was in the hold, swinging sometimes from the coamings as if I was hanging to a trapeze! We must keep her light at all costs. We had killed a lot of rock-birds, and, with the water and what not, began throwing them overboard. Then once I looked up to see how the Skipper was doing. There he was, calm as ever. But as I looked I saw him lean over with his left hand—like that—and pull something up out of the sea. Do you know what it was? One of the birds we had thrown over! He leant sideways a second time. Another bird! He did not know we had pitched them out. He thought they had got washed overboard, and he wasn't losing anything while the going was still possible!" You could see the wild scene in the eye of the younger speaker, the scene and that touch of the fantastic, the incredible, that made us both laugh.

A voice came to the hatch and shouted down, "A French smack!" The Skipper at once went on deck. I was trying to make up my mind to follow him, when one of the crew descended the short ladder and said we should be there in half an hour. And the French smack? "She's disappearing round towards the big island. She's poaching lobsters." He smiled.

There was no sign of the French smack when I got on deck, but here were the Flannan Isles, and I gazed at their great rock faces and green crests with some awe.

Outposts in the Atlantic, they had about them that air of the remote and wild, shut off by incalculable seas, sustaining the shock of thunderous water, pierced by the myriad screaming birds, and haunted by an unhuman loneliness that has to be felt to be dimly understood.

To most people who know of the Flannans there is also added the tragedy of the lighthouse, that unsolved mystery of the sea. It arrests thought now and holds it in an emotion timeless and static as the rocks themselves.

But the moment had come for action, as we nosed into the swinging waters between the cliff walls of the two islands to the south of the big island (Eilean Mór). An anchor went overboard for'ard, and we slid in slowly stern first to the rock on our right. With a foot on the stern-post, and gripping a three-pronged light anchor or grappling-iron with rope attached, one of the lads got ready. On the heave of the waters the boat rose and fell six or eight feet. Some three or four yards off-shore, he threw the grappling-hook on to the rock ledges and pulled, but the hook came away. Not until he had tried many times did one of the prongs catch in a crevice and hold. The stern was brought nearer the rock. Then, about a yard away (for we dared not go nearer), as the stern came up, he leapt—and landed, grabbing and holding on to the rock. The remaining two Kenneths and Alastair followed one after the other, leaping across the narrow aperture of deep sea that boiled under their feet. They looked up the broken cliff face and began to climb. It was steep enough, but manifestly not impossible for anyone with a sound head. Besides, they knew the way, and slipped along sideways under a projecting bluff, and round, and up and on. Presently they entered the region of a very green vegetation, white with what appeared to be blossom, and in a short time after that had gone out over the top.

"Will they bring the sheep down there?" I asked.

"Oh yes," said the Skipper. "This is the easiest place."

"How many?"

"We put six on to it this time last year, but that's not to say they will be there now."

"Do they fall over sometimes?"

"Yes. But—— I don't know. I wouldn't say that the rock is

always to blame." He smiled in his quiet way. It occurred to me that a fishing-vessel after days, or perhaps weeks, at sea might not be altogether averse to some fresh meat.

Our conversation was interrupted by distant shouts, and in a moment we saw the heads of sheep tossed up against the skyline. The beasts came on, and the four men appeared, whooping and flailing their arms in terrifying style. As the slow advance down the rocks proceeded, how I regretted that I could not use my camera, for it was now nine o'clock at night, and the light, under the grey sky, was hopeless for taking photographs.

"There are only four sheep?"

"Yes," answered the Skipper. "Only four." His voice and expression conveyed no slightest annoyance or regret. Two of his sheep had gone, and, apparently, that was that. The true attitude of the man born to the hazard of the sea. One felt there was no deliberate restraint or suppression. The attitude was natural. And, in fact, the loss was never again referred to.

After their year's residence on this island rock, the sheep were not only in splendid condition, with wool of an unbelievable cleanness, but as nimble on their feet as goats. There was more than one exciting moment when a beast all but broke back from the edge through the cordon. Then a man leapt in a way that rivalled the sheep, while one hand grabbed and let fly a sod—flower, root, and earth. The aim was always accurate and convinced the sheep without hurting it. We laughed when at one critical moment a squawking puffin was hurled through the air. For all this was taking place directly above us and to the accompaniment of a thousand screaming birds. They squatted on their inaccessible ledges; they darkened the air. Puffins, fulmars, guillemots, razorbills, petrels, gulls, kittiwakes, cormorants, they all nest here.

This was no reconstruction of the past, as one sometimes sees it on a film. The Skipper actually paid rent for the grazing on these rocks. This was part of his livelihood. Yet, as a "shot", it

certainly impressed me more than anything of the kind I had
ever seen in a cinema.

Down the broken rock to the ledges, the overhanging bluffs,
directly above the boat, until the sheep had to be persuaded to
go the last and only way. And, after a final dangerous break,
they went, until they were penned on the last ledge of all. The
boat was drawn in until, in that heaving sea, its stern-post was
clearing the rock by the narrowest permissible margin. Then a
sheep was caught and, as the boat rose, heaved at the man on the
stern-post, who caught it and swung it on board.

When all four sheep were thus loaded, the reverse process
started. One by one six sheep were thrown at the two men on
the ledge, who caught them and set them on their way up the
rocks. They had, in fact, to climb after them, pushing them on
in front, until the green vegetation was reached. Whereupon
the lads gave a last shout for luck and turned back. I watched
the sheep. Their consternation was obvious. One looked at the
green stuff—and tried it vaguely. Before we pushed off from
that rock, all six were busily browsing, while they slowly
climbed.

"But you can't go up there!" I exclaimed, as the boat slid in
stern first to the rock wall of the opposite island.

Yes, they could to-day, but not always. If the rock was wet,
for example, the feet would get no hold. Though, even then,
they had seen themselves use a scarf or other garment for treading on. "It's worse than it looks from the boat", one of them
assured me out of a long experience of the black and often
treacherous surface.

The grappling-hook was thrown about a dozen times before
at last it got what seemed to me a very precarious grip. The
boat was eased in as near as possible, and, as she rose from the
plunge, the oldest Kenneth leapt—and landed. I began to feel
uncomfortable. The others followed him. The rock above them

was a sheer black wall, but a narrow ledge, sloping to the sea, ran to their left and gave on a miniature funnel. One after another, without any hesitation, they went nimbly along the dangerous ledge and climbed up the funnel—and thus in a few minutes the worst of it was over, though we watched them for a long time hauling themselves up over the broken surfaces above.

"How many have you here?"

"Three," said the Skipper. "Though I'm only expecting two, because one of them was ailing."

"As no poacher would think of tackling that rock, perhaps you'll get all three!" I suggested.

He smiled back. "Perhaps so," he said.

Looking at the sheer rock, one could not help reflecting: for three sheep! Even much less than that: one year's growth on three sheep—with a possible loss of a whole sheep! One could hardly help an involuntary, if unspoken, tribute to this Skipper and these men. What grand company they were—willing, good-natured, courteous, and full of pluck!

Here was the other side to that dark picture of the "dole" and all it was supposed to represent in economic inefficiency and lack of initiative. What a sad mess had been made of Highland economics! How tragic the misunderstanding of what was not merely an economic problem but a whole way of living!

I thought of the grumbling of southern farmers, whose dogs moved a thousand sheep from one fenced pasture to another.

In his blood the true Highlander is still a hunter and a seaman. Twenty-four hours on end he will stand incredible discomfort and danger if all his energies are employed, if life gets its thrill from continuous movement with a definite object in view. But he has got to live, and if the result of his labours does not amount to the certainty of "dole" payments that can be got without such labours, naturally, being human, he is inclined to take, like the rest of us, the easiest and safest economic way out.

We heard the shouts. They were coming. Far above us we saw—three sheep, one as sturdy and nimble as another.

"They're all there!"

"Ay," said the Skipper.

A game in persuasion! Each sheep took a hurried yard or two and stood; a yard or two and stood; glancing to right and left; anxious to break back, but terrified of the leaping noisy humans behind. They could still go another yard or two . . .

"There's one island round the back there—we'll go to it next time—that is very difficult," said the Skipper. "Do you see that ledge away up there on the right? Well, it was like that, only worse. A sheep went right on to it and stuck there, and nothing that the boys could do would make it move. It was just big enough to hold the sheep and it was right over the sea." Seventy feet of a drop, I judged, into a boiling sea (with a possible knock on the bulge of the rock midway). "Well, at last Alastair climbed down on to the ledge itself and gripped the sheep, and after a little struggle he got it up."

This story reminded me of my rebellious stomach, and I certainly did not want to be a spectator of any such feat at the moment. Fortunately, nothing untoward happened. Men and sheep came down the funnel together and along the treacherous ledge. Three sheep were heaved out, persuaded along the ledge, and up the funnel.

"Did you ever have an accident?"

"Never, I am happy to say," replied the Skipper.

And so we left that dark rock and made for our last landing, the island with the lighthouse, for it was the largest of the Flannan group and would take the remainder of our cargo, over twenty sheep.

The Light that Failed

We were approaching the east landing, and already on the cement stairs that had been set in the living rock we could see two figures from the Flannan lighthouse. The cliffs on the east side of Eilean Mór attain a height of some 300 feet. The top is a green tableland sloping to the west, where the height above sea-level is but 200 feet. We could now see the crane on a hewn platform in the face of the rock far above high-water mark. Its long white arm is used for hoisting merchandise and, occasionally, human beings in slings from the deck of the relief ship. For the greater part of the year there is probably no other way by which a man could get landed on this island. But the swell was not so bad to-night, even if the light was fading, and we stood in stern first in the usual manner.

Our rope was now caught by expert hands. Our leading seaman leapt on to the cement steps, nimbly avoiding the swirls of water, and in a few moments unloading the remainder of the sheep we had brought from Bernera began. One by one they started to mount the steps that slanted up the face of the cliff. Occasionally a beast left the steps and tried an advance upon the precipice itself, but after a yard or two had to admit defeat. It was a laborious business, and I thought we were lucky to get them all landed without mishap. The Skipper suggested I should go up and see the lighthouse, so I waited for the plunging stern to come up, leapt for the concrete step, and slid on its slime a successful yard. The Skipper and Alastair remained behind to look after the boat.

We were all invited to his home by the friendly quiet-mannered head lighthouse-keeper, but on the way up we wondered whether it would not be wiser first of all to collect our sheep and get them on board. The daylight was going fast, for it must now have been after eleven o'clock, and though it would not get quite dark, still, there were three or four hours ahead when it would certainly be darker. While the hunt started I was invited up to see the lens.

A lighthouse has always had a peculiar attraction for me. In earliest boyhood I could count on a clear night seven flashes across a wide sea. And now and then, in later years, the image of the lighthouse has come into mind. As the great prismatic sphere slowly revolves it throws over the dark waters its beam of light. Impartially it shines forth, like sun or moon. Indeed, it is when sun and moon and all the stars are gone in a roaring blackness that it takes their place and, in its smaller orbit, fulfils their directing purpose with equal certainty. It is then, as the flashes cross a skipper's eyes and he counts and times them, that he learns where he is, and thereupon proceeds with confidence into the tempestuous night.

On top of the ladder I sat looking at the bright globe that revolved with slow steadfastness. I looked around me and out upon a darkening world. Cleanliness, and order, and discipline, and—light.

I came out of the lighthouse to find men and sheep rushing

through the gloom as in a mimic battle, converging on those hundreds of cement steps that zigzagged down the cliff. And at last a sheep broke through! A figure pursued at full tilt, but, as it turned out, the sheep won. It took a fair time to heave the many sheep on deck, for the boat was plunging a lot, as if the swell had increased. Once I thought I saw a sheep in the surf after an unsuccessful heave (these beasts were much heavier than those we had brought over), but in the end they were got safely on board; and this, everything taken into account, in the deep gloom of that midnight, was a remarkable enough feat.

The crew relaxed, wiping their foreheads, and when the hospitable head of the lighthouse suggested that a cup of tea or coffee might be refreshing, we did not disagree but there and then turned and began climbing again the multitude of steps— all, that is, except the Skipper and Alastair, who, well content with the night's exertions, stuck to the *Rhoda*. As for the single sheep that had won a temporary respite, it would be duly collected on the next trip.

After being hospitably entertained, we came out again into the night, all feelings of exertion or strain gone in the mood of ease and relaxation. The crying of the sea-birds in the cliffs seemed to have increased. I could hear the continuous booming of the sea. Then the whole atmosphere of the place seeped inward in that darkness that was faint with light, and there was born the emotion of an ultimate loneliness, as if one stood on a storm-lashed outpost of the world.

I looked up at the light. Day and night a man was on duty there. Every half-hour the mechanism was wound up that kept the great crystal globe revolving. In calm and tempest, its beam swept over the dark seas. The light that never failed. And then I remembered that once the light had failed.

The Skipper had told me how one night over in Uig, in Lewis, a gamekeeper could not see the light. But, perhaps, the atmosphere was thick outside? For how could the light fail? The following night—there was no light. It was mid-December in the year 1900. The absence of the light was reported, and on the 26th of December the Northern Lighthouse steamer drew in towards the east landing. Once a month, if weather permitted, this steamer visited the lighthouse with whatever gear or provisions were required, and landing one man, took another off, for the men worked on a continuous shift of two months on the island and one off. But now there was no sign of life about the lighthouse, no response to the steamer's signal, and, as a small boat was lowered and got away, there were no figures on the steps.

It was not difficult to imagine the scene, even to experience in some measure, not only the concern and trepidation, but that deeper eerier emotion of insecurity that invades the mind at such a moment. Up those cement steps, up the narrow double line of rail by which heavy goods are hauled to the store, up the bare slope in front, up to the lighthouse itself, white and silent.

They searched the lighthouse, but found no one. The last entry in the log-book was made at 9 a.m. on the 15th of December. The morning's work had been completed. The lamps were trimmed and charged. The lenses had been polished. All was shipshape and in order. They searched the outhouses, searched every corner of the island, but no trace of them has ever been found. Why and how they disappeared must now for ever remain one of the mysteries of the sea.

There are one or two theories. In the living-room there was evidence of a hastily interrupted breakfast. One chair had been knocked back. Apparently something had called the men's attention urgently. On the three nights preceding the 15th, the log-book shows that a tremendous gale had been blowing from the west. It has been suggested that the mind of one of the men gave way under the strain, that he got up precipitately and made for the cliff, that the two others followed him, and, in the final struggle, all three went over.

But this is very unlikely, because lighthouse-keeping implies a certain temperament to begin with, and, anyway, by the morning of the 15th the gale had blown itself out. There would still, of course, be terrific seas running; but the wearing roar of the wind, and, indeed, the danger of being swept over the cliffs by the sheer force of that wind, had gone.

The evidence in which our Skipper believes—and no man living knows these seas as he does—was collected round the west landing. At the east landing there was no trace of any violence from the storm. But at the west landing, against which the storm had smashed, there had been a remarkable happening. Some 112 feet above sea-level, a wooden box firmly fixed in a cranny of the rocks, and holding ropes, crane handles, and other gear, had been smashed open and its contents scattered far and wide.

Even in calm weather, this western coast knows these tremendous swells. The Skipper had lost his previous boat by just such a swell invading his normally secure anchorage at the inner end of a Bernera inlet. Many yards above high-water mark the brimming water rose, converting for the moment a land knoll into an island, before it receded yards beyond low-water mark, setting up in the process a whirling motion. In the course of the night this miniature maelstrom had, by spinning the vessel round, fouled the two anchor-chains and thrown her upon the rocks, where she was broken up.

And what was a sheltered narrow Bernera inlet compared with these rocks in this open sea? And that, after a three-day gale of terrific intensity! The lighthouse had only been established a year. The men would not know all the ways and currents of the ocean against the rock formations. In fact, subsequent observation proved that in calm weather the sea can pile itself up in a sudden and treacherous manner against the west landing.

The crane was some forty feet below the box and seventy feet above the sea. After the reverberating impact from a vast wave, the men may have hurried to the landing and, descending the steps, tried to collect their gear. A new wave comes sweeping towards them, to be thrown by the formation of the rocks into a climbing, upreaching mountain of green water. We know that one such wave reached over 112 feet. And we know that nothing living could at a lower level hang on when its immense mass and weight broke upon the cliff.

As I walked down the slope with the head keeper at the darkest hour of the night (it was now one o'clock in the morning), we came on the narrow-gauge rail that disappeared towards the west landing. It was hardly the time and the place to introduce the subject of the mystery of the Flannans.

"Do you use the west landing much?" I asked casually.

"Not much," he answered. "There are nasty swells there."

We made no other allusion to it. But one thing he did say, which I shall remember. I can hardly think that I would make the banal remark that it was lonely here or ask him if he felt lonely. Perhaps it was out of some momentary community of mood that he said, "No, I cannot say that I ever feel lonely. I like it." And I felt, rightly or wrongly, that I understood him.

Above the crying of the sea-birds and the booming of the waves, there was a feeling of the loneliness that has peace at its heart. For perhaps loneliness can be a terrifying thing, in itself, only to him who fears his own company. But to him who has no such fear, loneliness may bring peace and, on occasion, a quiet exaltation.

It may have been some such conception of loneliness and peace that drew the old Celtic missionaries of the early church to exactly such outposts as Eilean Mór. Indeed, the Flannan group are named after St. Flannan, an Irish saint of the seventh century, who is believed by tradition to have lived for years on Eilean Mór. The ruins of his simple oratory may be seen behind the lighthouse.

An arm was ready to catch us as we leapt from the slippery step to the stern-post, after having bade the men of the lighthouse good-bye. Out into the open sea and the plunge and roll of the heavy cross-swell. How steadfast looked the lighthouse on its black wall of rock, how serene its beam! For many a mile it would accompany us through the night.

"You'll be more comfortable below," said the Skipper. "It's getting very cold."

So we went down, and the Skipper lowered a berth that had been hinged against the boat's side. The simple mattress, being rarely used these days, added a faint odour of mildew to the atmosphere, but its dampness bred a gradual warmth and comfort. I took off my oilskins and lay on my back. The Skipper, on the other side, did not lower his bunk, but merely stretched himself on the hard board of the seat. For a long time we smoked and talked. Once or twice one of us went up on deck to see how the lads were getting on. They were crowded behind a wind-shelter, with the compass before them. None of them appeared to have a thought of turning in, though there were four good bunks in the den.

"It's cosy here," I said.

Yes, many a night he had spent in this small space; and many a night in the dens of fishing boats on many seas. It was fine to listen to him talking in his quiet pleasant voice. But the picture that sticks most vividly in my mind concerns these same Flannan rocks, when Alastair and himself used to go lobster-fishing there on the *Rhoda* in the depth of winter. Sometimes it would be icy cold, and the sea, as one could imagine, would hardly be very smooth. Hauling and cleaning and baiting the lobster-pots was a bitterly cold job. In truth, often it would freeze you to the marrow. But when the work was over, *then* to come down into the den here, with its warm fire, and settle in for the night, while the boat herself rode the elements, ah, it was homely and fine!

One could feel the warmth of it, the companionship of men in hard and dangerous toil. Long thoughts about it drifted through the mind. The inshore fishing, surely the most natural way of fishing, had to a large degree been ruined by economic causes beyond the power of these fishermen to control. Economic causes? Let us have moments of human companionship when even to discuss profit-hunting and greed may be forgotten. Let us listen to one another's voices in the den of a small boat on a stormy sea. There is a chance then that human values may be seen in reasonable perspective; there is a certainty that the mystery of human life, and the companionship and goodness that so miraculously come out of it, will at least be perceived. The rotten bait slips back into the sea.

We dozed, and spoke, and sometimes one of the crew came down to get a warming. The sky was black and it was keeping very dark, but soon they should be picking up the land.

We picked up the land, and presently were in the tumult round Gallan Head. After the pranks that had been played by my internal economy, there had supervened a certain bodiless feeling that was by no means unpleasant. The clock had made a double round since we had gazed expectantly at Alastair's cow, but it seemed a longer stretch of time than that.

Two or three miles more, and we ran into the shelter of the island of Pabaidh Mhór, into a calm sea with white sands on the Lewis shore. The morning was now advanced, but no smoke came from croft cottages, and the land lay still and strangely fresh under the grey sky. Often summer mornings in this western world have to a marked degree this curiously arrested air of enchantment. After long physical toil or endurance, the mind, too, at such a moment is conscious of release from the body and all its desires, all its urgent moods. The voice goes quiet, and the spirit floats in an air of friendliness and fellowship. Strife seems an odd phenomenon, a madness of the uncleansed flesh, and the thought of it, in the abstract, is something to smile at.

The Promised Land

One final picture of the Skipper.

When with our cargo of sheep from the Flannan Isles we at last stood in to the Lewis shore near Breascleit, we found a shallow shelving bottom, brown with heavy seaweed. Fouling a small propeller is all too easy, so after the Skipper had said, in that tone of voice which seems to carry a friendly suggestion rather than an order, "That will do fine," we stopped the *Rhoda* some thirty yards short of the beach.

But by this time one has learned not to rush in with the foolish question. Time will disclose what is going to happen next, though I admit I wondered how on earth we were going to land our living cargo here. The matter presented no difficulty to the Skipper. He simply caught a sheep fore and aft, lifted it over the gunnel and dropped it in the sea. From the sinking splash the sheep buoyed up, keeping the nostrils high over a closed mouth. And then an extraordinary thing happened: after swimming round in a very small circle, the sheep struck back for the boat.

During the long night and morning I had sometimes wondered how the sheep were getting on, for our passage across that sea of the high hurtling waves and the wide deep troughs had given the *Rhoda* a smoothly complicated motion where up-and-down goes onwards and sideways at the same time, and, down below, goes backwards as well. If ever there had been a prison beyond the understanding of sheep, the hold of the *Rhoda* had surely been that prison to those sheep.

Yet here was the grey fleecy beast, with uptilted nostrils and with eyes on the tall bearded Skipper, who looked at that moment like a patriarchal prophet, here it came cutting the water with sharp forefeet in an anxiety to get back to the prison fold.

The Skipper stooped and lifted the boathook, got an end of it gently behind the sheep's head, and slowly turned the head towards the shore. "Look—yonder", he said; the sheep looked and saw the green rise of the ground beyond the brown shore and struck out like one that had been given a vision of the promised land.